The Fisherman's Companion

THE FISHERMAN'S COMPANION

SECOND EDITION

Frank Holan

Illustrated by
Mary Villarejo

Alan C. Hood & Company, Inc.
CHAMBERSBURG, PENNSYLVANIA

TO JENNIFER
Because she is a
Rare Gem

ISBN 0-911469-15-X

Published by Alan C. Hood & Company, Inc.
Chambersburg, PA 17201

Copies of *The Fisherman's Companion*
may be obtained by sending $15.95 per copy to:

Alan C. Hood & Company, Inc.
P.O. Box 775
Chambersburg, PA 17201

Price includes postage and handling.
Quantity discounts are available to dealers
and non-profit organizations.
Write on letterhead for details.

Library of Congress Cataloging-in-Publication Data
Holan, Frank.
    The Fisherman's Companion / Frank Holan : illustrated by Mary
Villarejo. -- 2nd ed.
        p.   cm.
    Includes bibliographical references (p.145).
    ISBN 0-911469-15-X (paperback)
    1. Fishing.   I. Title
SH441.H7   1999
799.1--dc21   99-27990
                                                         CIP

Table of contents

Now for the art of catching *fish, that is to say, how
to make a man – that was none – to be an angler
by a book; he that undertakes it shall undertake a
harder task than* Mr. Hales *(a most valiant and
excellent fencer) who, in a printed book called* A
Private School of Defence, *undertook to teach that
art or science, and was laughed at for his labour.
Not but that many useful things might be learnt by
that book, but he was laughed at because that art
was not to be taught by words, but practise; and so
must angling. And note also, that in this Discourse,
I do not undertake to say all that is known, or may
be said of it, but I undertake to acquaint the reader
with many things that are not usually known to
every angler; and I shall leave gleanings and obser-
vations enough to be made out of the experience of
all that love and practise this recreation, to which I
shall encourage them. For* angling *may be said to
be so like the* mathematics, *that it can never be fully
learnt; at least not so fully, but that there will still be
more new experiments left for the trial of other men
that succeed us.*

—Izaak Walton,
The Compleat Angler,
Notice to the Reader

FOREWORD

Most instructional primers on any subject are dreary things, as joyful to read as a translated manual on assembling something like an outdoor gas grill. Reading them after supper or a substantial lunch is a ticket to near instantaneous postprandial slumber. Oh, they give you the information you need but where's the fun?

Frank Holan's *Fisherman's Companion* is fun. Though its purpose is to take anyone who has developed an interest in sportfishing and knows nothing of it, from ground zero to at least functioning angler level, there'll be no nodding off along the way. Holan's lessons, history and philosophy are intelligent, delightfully witty, insightful and practical. Along with helping you select the tackle best for your purposes and learn to use it, you'll begin to understand why fish do what they do, and how to exploit that knowledge to catch them with every kind of equipment from lures to natural baits (including the potent maggot, though it cleverly hides behind a *nom de guerre*).

Holan's take on conservation issues doesn't fudge when it comes to real problems of overpopulation and destructive human practices. But far from being the usual hand-wringer, he makes a case for you to understand angling as a kind of life allegory that just may lead you to some physical good works. Good stuff to ponder, and a good volume to have on hand afloat or on the stream bank should the fish happen not to be biting.

—Jerry Gibbs,
Fishing Editor,
Outdoor Life.

PREFACE

Any idiot can catch fish, if you interpret the word "catch" rather loosely. During World War II, when scarcity of food in much of Western Europe coincided with lots of war materiel lying around loose, any hungry citizen lucky enough to get hold of a hand grenade had only to pull the pin and throw it into the nearest stream. The grenade would explode; all the fish within the radius of a certain number of feet would either be killed or stunned by the concussion, and would float to the surface, from which they could easily be scooped up. Of course, if enough people did this often enough, most types of fish in the kind of water in question would become scarce, and some might even become extinct, so it is no wonder that in most places this type of fishing is against the law.

At any rate, this is not what this book is all about.

If you did a lot of research, borrowed a lot of money, invested in a fleet of trawlers (complete with nets, winches, refrigerated holds, and sonar equipment), registered with the appropriate authorities, lined up a market for your output, hired a bunch of workers with the right skills and experience, and turned them loose, you could probably catch fish too, and at the end of the year you could total it all up and find out whether you earned or lost money.

This is not what this book is about either.

A good many millennia ago, some cave-man genius, whose name is lost to history (if he had a name at all) found out that if you tied a sharp sliver of stone or bone to a string, impaled a piece of meat on the sliver, and let

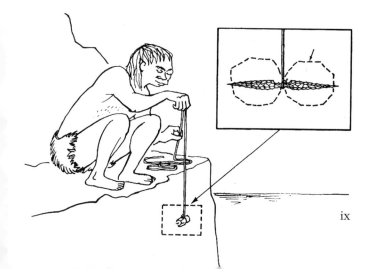

both sliver and meat down into a body of water inhabited by fish, it sometimes happened that a fish, attempting
to swallow the meat, would get the sliver stuck in his
throat, and could be hauled out. Every once in a while
samples of this type of contraption, known by archaeolo-
gists as a "gorge," are found by scientists interested in digging up and studying that sort of thing.

The trouble with the gorge was that, because of its
structure, sometimes it would work and sometimes it
wouldn't, so, several millennia later, another anonymous
cave-man genius improved on the basic model by inventing the hook. It wasn't quite as elegant as a modern
hook–after all, metallurgy had not yet been invented–but
it was based on the same general principle, and apparently worked fairly well. Anyway, the process of combining hooks with something fish can be expected to strike
at (bait or artificial lures), tying them on the ends of lines,
and tossing them into waters which can reasonably be
expected to contain fish has been going on ever since.

In terms of protein harvested versus capital and/or
manhours expended, the process is grossly inefficient,
but, for some reason, many otherwise sane people, even
today, indulge in it with more enthusiasm that it would
seem to warrant–they claim to find it soothing. It has been
suggested that this is due to atavism–the pleasure we feel
today when we land a fish is a survival of the fierce joy of
countless generations of cave-men realizing that death by
starvation had been postponed for at least a few days; at
the same time, we are somewhat better off than the cave-
man, in that the disappointment we feel when they aren't
biting is tempered by the reflection that there is plenty of
hamburger in the refrigerator.

Maybe so, maybe not; anyway, this is what this book is
all about.

1. Rods & Reels

Visitors to Alaska sometimes notice Eskimo children, some of them quite small, sitting for hours next to a hole in the ice, fishing. Their equipment consists of nothing more than a hand-held line, a hook on the end of the line, and some sort of bait or other type of fish-attractor–a small piece of cloth, or a pearl button–on or near the hook. They catch fish, too.

However, hand-held lines have two drawbacks: in the first place, they severely restrict the area of water in which you can operate, and, in the second place, if the fish hooked is capable of exerting considerable force, there is a good possibility that the line will be broken or the hook will tear loose. When the Old Man, in Hemingway's *The Old Man and the Sea*, had hooked a big sailfin on a hand-held line, he did not dare tie the line to a stanchion and go to sleep; he had to stand in the bows for several days, with the line across his back, so that if the fish suddenly decided to jerk at the line, he could cushion the force of the jerk with his body and prevent the fish from breaking loose.

Using a pole or rod goes far toward solving both of these problems–not only can you cover a much bigger expanse of water; you can also be fairly sure that as long as you keep the rod more or less at right angles to the probable direction of the pull, whenever a fish tugs suddenly at the line, the rod will yield without letting go, automatically absorbing a good deal of the force of the tension exerted.

Some people have the idea that a cane pole is hopelessly old-fashioned, hopelessly inefficient, or for some other reason unworthy of a true fisherman. This is an illusion. (For an account of how, under certain circumstances, a cane pole can be not only as good as any other kind of fishing rig, but considerably superior, read Chapter 5 of *30 Miles for Ice Cream*, by Murray Hoyt.) However, it must be admitted that for most purposes, a cane pole is less versatile than a rod provided with some sort of reel from which line can be unwound.

For anglers using rod-and-reel combinations, the four commonest are: bait-casting, spin-casting, spinning, and fly rods. There is a certain amount of latitude in the weights these types can effectively handle, but in general, bait-casting rods are for use with heavy lures; spin-casting and spinning rods, with medium-weight lures; and fly rods, with flies and other lures of practically no weight at all.

Most bait-casting, spin-casting, spinning, or fly rods nowadays are made of hollow fiberglass, but you can still get split-bamboo fly rods if you are willing to pay enough for them. It is a curious fact that the cheapest pole and the most expensive fly rod are both made of the same basic material. The difference in price is based on the fact that whereas the bamboo pole is used just as it is found in nature, the bamboo fly rod is made up of six split triangular sections, meticulously fitted and glued together.

A relatively new phenomenon that may eventually replace bamboo as the most prestigious fly-rod material has appeared on the market: the fly rod of hardened graphite. It is stronger and lighter than either bamboo or fiberglass, and its particular kind of flexibility somehow makes possible the attainment of considerably greater ranges than bamboo or fiberglass can deliver. I wouldn't rush right out and buy one, though, unless I were feeling pretty flush–they don't come cheap.

While we are on the subject of new developments, we might as well mention rod guides. Guides for bait-casting and spinning rods are all circular, but fly rods are a little special–the one on the fisherman end is circular and of medium size; the one on the tip is also circular, and somewhat smaller; all the rest are "snake guides," guides made in the form of a lazy spiral, which has been shown to be the shape that will best accommodate fly-line action. Most rod guides are of plain metal, but the rearmost and tip guides of some of the newer fly rods are inset with a ring of aluminum oxide, which, like Teflon, has the property of reducing friction to practically nothing.

It is not likely that anybody ever learned how to get the lure out to where the fish are merely by reading a book; however, text and diagrams do help the fisherman sort out in his own mind the steps necessary to operate his particular tackle, especially if he takes the further step of trying it out in the back yard. Some authorities–mostly fly fishermen–don't approve of dry-land practice, but I can't see any harm in it: it seems to me that it is more reasonable for the aspirant to work on the acquisition of the necessary motor skills *before* he finds himself on the water, with additional complications, like wind, weather, and the clever remarks of companions, or even uninvited kibitzers, to distract him. Tackle shops sell or give away little tear-drop-shaped gadgets that serve as practice lures, but any small object of the appropriate weight will do. Fly rods of course need no weight at all. (Note: Be sure to use the proper line–see Chapter 2.)

BAIT-CASTING

A bait-casting reel is one with a spool which revolves as line is stripped off it:

Most bait-casting reels nowadays are equipped with a level-wind mechanism: the line passes through the slot or eyelet of a contraption that moves back and forth, distributing the line evenly on the spool.

Some bait-casting reels are also equipped with a slipping clutch arrangement known as a star drag, so called because of the shape of its adjusting lever. (It actually looks more like a five-pointed asterisk.) Its purpose is to prevent the line from breaking if subjected to sudden strain. If the star drag is set properly, whenever the tension on the line approaches the point at which the line would normally break, the clutch slips, the reel gives up a certain amount of line, and the tension is relieved.

A bait-casting rig is a little tricky to operate. By flipping the tip of the rod forward, you send the lure sailing out over the water; the weight of the lure makes the spool revolve, unwinding line as it goes. So far, so good. But sooner or later, the lure will lose forward momentum and stop; if you fail to jam your thumb against the spool soon enough, the spool will keep on merrily turning long after the lure has stopped, forming what is known to the initiate as a "bird's nest"–a wad of madly tangled line like you wouldn't believe; but if you jam your thumb against the spool *too* soon, the lure, arrested in mid-career, will bounce back at least part of the way between you and the place where the lure was supposed to land. Anyway, this is the way it works:

1. With the lure two or three inches beyond the tip of

the rod, and your thumb pressed against the line on the spool to keep it from revolving, hold the rod in front of you at an angle of about 45° from the ground.

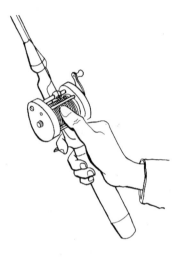

2. Move the rod, briskly but not desperately, no farther back than the point at which the rod seems to be pointing straight up in the air ...

3. . . . and immediately whip the rod forward, simultaneously releasing your thumb.

4. As forward motion of the lure slows, clamp your thumb down again, to prevent backlash and the formation of the aforementioned bird's nest.

5. Change the rod to your left hand and turn the crank to retrieve.

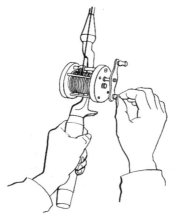

Notice in Step Two that the rod only *seems* to be pointing up in the air. It doesn't, because, since you have suddenly stopped its backward career, the momentum provided by its own weight (to say nothing of the weight of the lure) has bent it into an arc, building up static energy that you convert into kinetic energy as you flip the rod forward. If it didn't do this, you might as well use a broomstick furnished with reel and guides.

Bait-casting fanatics don't simply whip the rod forward and clamp down the thumb when the lure has started to lose momentum. In order to hit a precise spot on the water, they flip the rod forward with a bit more power than absolutely necessary, and as the lure nears the goal they "feather" the line–apply just enough thumb pressure to slow the lure down so it falls where it is supposed to fall. A surprising amount of precision can be achieved in this way.

SPIN-CASTING

As we have seen, the bait-casting reel is something of a contradiction in terms: on one hand, if the spool fails to revolve freely, it won't work properly; on the other hand, the faster it revolves, the worse the bird's nest you will have if you don't stop the revolution soon enough. Somewhere along the line, some inventive fellow got to thinking about how to resolve the difficulty, and came up with the Fixed-Spool Principle.

If you stand an ordinary spool of thread on one of its ends, grab the end of the thread, and pull upward, chances are that the thread will come off the spool readily enough. In the same way, a line wound on to the spool of a properly-designed reel mounted endwise, rather than sidewise, on a rod, if pulled from the tip end of the rod, will come off the spool in much the same way. The spool does not revolve; it just sits there.

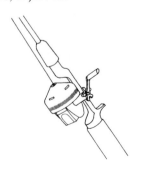

The spin-casting reel uses the Fixed-Spool Principle.

Of the four processes we have mentioned, spin-casting is undoubtedly the easiest to learn. It works like this:

1. With the lure two or three inches beyond the tip of your rod, and your thumb on the button, hold the rod in front of you at an angle of about 45° from the ground.

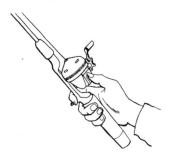

2. Move the rod briskly no farther back than the point at which the rod seems to be pointing straight up in the air . . .

3. . . . and immediately whip the rod forward, simultaneously releasing your thumb.

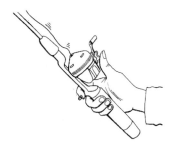

4. When the lure has landed, change the rod to your left hand and turn the crank to retrieve.

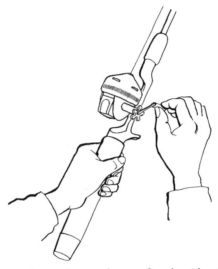

Some spin-casting reels are fitted with star drags; in others, slipping-clutch devices are activated by adjusting the position of the nose cone.

SPINNING

The spinning reel also uses the Fixed-Spool Principle, but differs from the spin-casting reel in several ways: (1) the spool, instead of being concealed by a hood, is clearly visible; (2) the spool is mounted under, rather than on top of, the rod; and (3) the crank is turned with the left, rather than the right, hand.

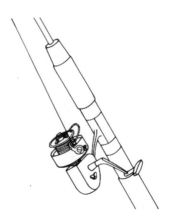

The term Fixed-Spool as applied to the spinning reel is not absolutely accurate–although the spool does not revolve, in most models it does move up and down slightly as the crank is turned, in order to distribute the line evenly on the spool, somewhat as a level-wind mechanism distributes line evenly on the spool of a bait-casting reel.

Spinning is almost as easy to learn as spin-casting. It works like this:

1. With the lure two or three inches beyond the tip of your rod, and holding the rod in front of you at an angle of about 45° from the ground, turn the bail to Open position, and engage the line with the right forefinger.

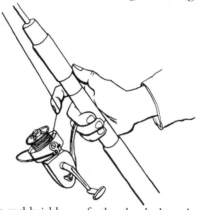

2. Move the rod briskly no farther back than the point at which the rod seems to be pointing straight up in the air ...

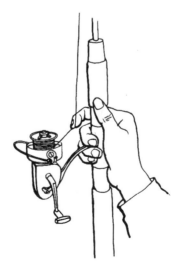

3. ...and immediately whip the rod forward, simultaneously releasing the line by pointing your forefinger at the place where the lure is to land.

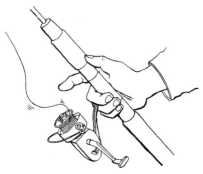

4. When the lure has landed, turn the crank to retrieve, using the *left* hand. You don't have to worry about the bail–the action of turning the crank will automatically flip the bail into Retrieve position.

Spinning rods are normally provided with slipping-clutch devices activated by adjusting the top plate of the reel.

FLY-ROD FISHING

Thus far we have been discussing methods of tossing out lures of various weights–comparatively heavy weights with bait-casting rods, and lighter lures with spin-casting and spinning rods. In fly-rod fishing, the lure is so light that it might as well not be there at all; it is the weight of the *line* that must get the source of enticement out to where the fish is.

A lot of authorities–real authorities, too, and not just armchair theorists–claim that fly fishing is not more difficult than any other kind of rod manipulation. Others claim it is. Regardless of whether the process is easy or difficult to learn, there isn't the slightest doubt that it is harder to describe in words. For one thing, you can't produce even a modest cast until you get some line straightened out in front of you, and by the time you are though describing how this is to be done, your explanation has sprouted so many whereases and howevers that it makes the exposition kind of hard to follow.

Perhaps the best way out is to describe what happens if you do your casting on dry land, and later extrapolate your knowledge backwards.

A fly reel, like a bait-casting reel, revolves as line is stripped off it. It has no star drag or other slipping-clutch device, and enters only passively into the casting process, being simply a mechanism on which to store line until it is needed.

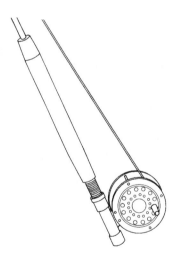

You can get automatic reels, incorporating a clock-work device that rewinds loose line onto the reel at the touch of a lever, but most fly fishermen seem to get along without them, and for the beginner they would probably pose more problems than they would solve. Fly rods work like this:

1. Lay a few feet of line out on the ground in front of you, pointing in the direction you are going to cast.

2. Holding the rod at an angle of about 45° from the ground, strip three or four coils of line off the reel, and hold them *loosely* in your left hand.

3. Move the rod briskly no farther back than the point at which you think the rod is pointing straight up in the air. (Actually, fly-rod purists recommend about 10° past straight up in the air, but until you get the hang of it, it is better to err in the direction of conservatism.)

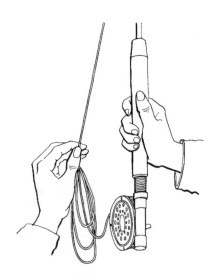

4. Wait until you can feel the weight of the line bending your rod; then, again with wrist motion, flip the rod forward. If your grip on the coils of line is loose enough, the weight of the part of the line moving away from your rod tip should pull at least some of the line out of your hand, and land the end of the line farther away from you than it was to begin with.

5. As the line is moving forward and downward, try to "ride the line down"–hold the rod at an angle of about 45° from the horizontal until you see the line beginning to fall, and then lower the rod-tip at the same speed as that of the falling line. (Fishermen who get into the habit of slapping the line masterfully down on the water catch few fish.)

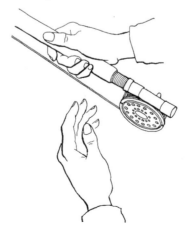

6. Change the rod to your left hand, and turn the crank to retrieve.

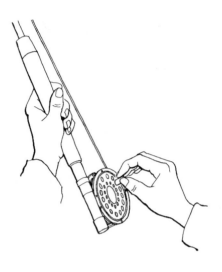

Well, that's the basic maneuver. Actual use in the field is a lot more complicated. For one thing, experienced fly fishermen make frequent use of the device known as "false casting." Since the amount of line that can be shot through the guides with one flip of the rod is limited, the fly fisherman does not usually let his line fall to the water after his first flip, but whips it back and forth several times, stripping off coils of line with his left hand between each flip, before finally laying the line down where he wants it to go.

Perhaps the one thing that gives fly-casting its reputation for difficulty is its need for accurate timing. When making a series of false casts, the more line the fisherman strips off and allows to shoot forward through the guides on one forward cast, the longer the active part of the line is, and hence the longer the waiting interval between the subsequent backcast and the following forward cast must be. The fisherman cannot assign any fixed value–one-half second, one second, or two seconds–to this interval; he must wait until the rod "feels right"–until all the line between the tip of the rod and the fly is stretched out straight behind him.

Whether the active part of the line is long or short,

 if the fly fisherman flips his rod forward *too soon*, before the line has been fully extended, the line will pile up on the water in front of him;

 if he flips his rod forward *too late*, after the line has not only extended fully but begun to fall, he will snag his fly in the shrubbery behind him;

if he flips his rod forward as soon as the line is fully extended, he will be casting properly.

* * * * *

No matter which of these methods–bait-casting, spin-casting, spinning, or fly-casting–is used, there are two faults which most beginners, and a surprisingly large number of old-timers, commit:

1. **Trying to make manipulation of the rod hard work.** Some fishermen have the idea that manipulating a rod is like shotputting–you have to exert every muscle of your body to the utmost to get the lure "out there." This is ridiculous. Many a toothless, tottery little old gent can toss a heavy plug as far as it needs to go because he knows that the rod is supposed to do most of the work, and will, if you give it half a chance. The tendency to use excessive body English is particularly disastrous with the fly rod–not only does it tire you out needlessly; it actually interferes with the proper presentation of the lure.

2. **Laying the rod too far back.** The human arm is so constructed that, when you are holding a rod as you would when fishing, it is actually easier to touch the ground *behind* you with the tip of your rod than to touch the ground in front of you. For this reason, it is extremely easy to "lay it on the cornfield" behind you when casting, which invariably interferes with efficient presentation of

the lure. The more flexible the rod used, the greater the interference. Even the bait-casting rod, the stiffest of them all, if whipped too far to the rear when casting, will occasionally hang the lure onto nearby trees; the spinning rod, somewhat more flexible, has a tendency to shoot the lure straight up in the air, whence it falls on the fisherman's head; and the fly rod, the most willowy of all, will invariably entangle your fly in the plant life twenty or so feet to your rear.

* * * * *

With all these different kinds of rods to choose from, where do you begin, and how far do you go?

Well, how far you go will depend on how avid an angler you will eventually become, and you probably won't know that until you have done some serious fishing, so the first question to solve is how to begin.

Personally, I'd start with some sort of rig incorporating the Fixed Spool Principle. Learning to manipulate this type of gear is not at all difficult, and for distance and accuracy it is hard to beat.

If you are going to invest in a rig employing the Fixed Spool Principle, you will have to make a choice between a spin-casting and a spinning outfit. With this in mind, it might be useful to review the history of fixed-spool reels.

As I remember it, shortly after World War II, all kinds of weird and unlikely contraptions incorporating the Principle appeared on the market; in the course of time, the grossly impractical ones were eliminated, leaving the field pretty much to the two types with which we are familiar. The essential difference between them is the manner in which the line is stripped off of, and wound onto, their reels. In the case of the spin-casting reel, this function is carried out by means of the innards of that cone-shaped line-deflector out of which the line emerges; in the case of the spinning reel, by a two-position bail, something like the bail (handle) of a water-bucket: in the Open position, it allows the line to run out freely, and in the Retrieve position, it allows the line to be wound back on the reel. The spin-casting reel is usually a little cheaper, and, because of its construction, it can be (and sometimes is) mounted on a standard bait-casting rod, but I tend to favor the spinning reel, at least in part because the friction between the reel and the line is probably less, and the rod with its underslung reel seems to be more pleasurably balanced. (Whether these are the real reasons, or whether I am simply prejudiced in favor of the Garcia Mitchell which has served me well for the past 15 or 20 years, I will never know.)

Assuming you have got yourself a fixed-reel rig and used it awhile, you may grow so fond of it you may never want to use any other type of equipment. However, despite its versatility, there is one thing it cannot do: it cannot deposit an artificial fly on the surface of the water in such a manner as to create the impression that the fly had fallen there accidentally. And so, if you eventually find that life holds no more savor for you if you are denied the opportunity for deceiving surface-feeding fish, your next purchase may be a fly rod.

Again, an angler who has been using a fly rod for awhile may never feel the need for further acquisitions. Some anglers get so enamored of their fly rods that they use them for tasks other than those for which they were originally designed, to include fishing for lunker bass with large streamer flies and tiny popping bugs. Lest anybody feel that such use puts undue strain on a frail and delicate mechanism, let him be disabused. If the fish is big and tough enough, the fisherman may be unable to hold him, which means that the fish will either break the line or haul the fisherman bodily into the water, but the rod itself is fairly safe. All fishing rods are more or less flexible, and the fly rod is the most flexible of all, so attempting to break a fly rod by tugging at the line fastened to the end of it is a little like trying to punch a hole through a trampoline–the very flexibility of the device makes it easy to bend but hard to break. If you really want to break a fiberglass rod, all you have to do is slam a car door on its tip, as many a careless fisherman has found to his sorrow.

For all the versatility of fixed-spool rigs and fly rods, supposing you somehow get the notion that you want to fish for record muskellunge. Muskellunge sometimes get to weigh as much as 60 pounds. A lure big enough to interest a fish that heavy is going to be heavy too, so you may find yourself putting out money for a bait-casting rod.

If you reach this point, you have run through all the basic types there are. This does not mean you are now prepared for any type of fishing on the face of the globe–there are other types (ultra-light rods of all descriptions, ultra-stubby rods for trolling, and so on) but they are all variations on the basic pattern.

One of the variations on the basic pattern that is good

to know about is the surf rod. What we have been discussing up to now pretty well covers any kind of freshwater fishing you are likely to be doing, but saltwater fishing introduces a new element–some varieties of seagoing fish get to be so big that there is not much point in trying for them with any but the most massive equipment. This does not mean that if you switch from freshwater to saltwater fishing, you *must* buy a new rod, or a whole new set of rods–*any rod you use for freshwater fishing can be used for saltwater fishing*, providing you take the trouble to wash it thoroughly with fresh water afterwards, to prevent corrosion. But for the big ones–that's something else again.

(Sometimes even the most massive of equipment isn't enough. When a charter boatman's client happens to hook onto a manta ray–the boatman does not hesitate to cut the line, because if he doesn't, it is probable that the ray will simply stroll off with his rod, reel, and possibly client.)

A surf rod is nothing more or less than an oversized bait-casting or spinning rod, constructed in such a way that you hold the rod in a two-handed grip for casting, something like chopping with a woodsman's axe. It is manipulated pretty much like its smaller prototype, except that:

1. The lures used are so heavy that it would be impractical to hold the rod in front of you with the lure dangling from it prior to casting; instead, the lure usually lies on the beach more or less *behind* you, and is tossed into the water with a single sweep.

2. The two-handed grip makes it impractical to cast directly overhead, and so the path of the rod-tip in casting is usually an arc about half-way between the horizontal and the vertical. (Try it with a broomstick, and you will see what I mean.) Accuracy in casting probably suffers somewhat because of this (although veteran surf-casters may deny it), but since you practically never see the fish you are casting to, and since they might be just about anywhere along the coast anyway, pinpoint accuracy is not critical.

2. Lines

As long as you stick to cane poles, just about any kind of stout cord will do for line, but as soon as you switch over to anything more complex, you will have to start being more discriminating, choosing line that will work well with the equipment in question.

Bait-casting reels require flexible line combining great strength with small diameter, so most bait-casting lines are made of braided synthetic material, usually nylon or dacron. (There are bait-casting reels especially designed to accommodate monofilament, but they are rare.)

The peculiar structure of **fixed-spool reels** demands a somewhat springier line, to insure that it will come off the reel easily, so virtually all fixed-spool reels nowadays are provided with nylon monofilament. When fixed-spool reels were still something of a novelty, the monofilament then on the market was sometimes a little *too* springy for comfort, and would leap off the spool in big coils, like bed-springs, but manufacturers eventually discovered how to reduce the stiffness to manageable proportions. When a coil of monofilament is labeled "limp," this actually means "stiff enough to be used on a fixed-spool reel, but limp enough not to cause trouble."

Monofilament and braided line are both graded in terms of "pound test," the number of pounds of tension they will support before breaking. This does not mean that to catch a 100-pound fish you need a 100-pound line. As a matter of fact, in addition to contests in which the object of the game is to catch the heaviest fish of a partic-ular variety, there are also contests in which the object of the game is to catch the heaviest fish of a particular variety using a line of the lowest possible pound test. (Any sporting goods store can supply details.) You can catch a fish weighing several times the pound-test limit of the line used because a fish in the water is practically weightless, and the only strain on the line takes place when he is actively trying to get away. (If you are curious to see how this works, procure a rod furnished with a 10-pound line, fasten the end of the line to a 60-pound child who can swim, and challenge him to escape to the opposite end of the pool. The process would work equally well with a 150-pound man, but grown-ups are harder to sweet-talk into playing games of this kind.)

Moreover, if your reel is fitted with a star drag or other form of slip clutch, and you have adjusted it properly, the fish, no matter how heavy or powerful, cannot break the line by means of a direct tug: as soon as the force of the tug starts to approach the breaking point of the line, the clutch will slip, and the tension will be relieved. Of course, if all the line on the reel is exhausted, or if the line gets caught on an underwater snag, the fish may be able to exert a direct pull on the line in excess of its pound-test rating, and hence escape.

Some fishermen believe that when old and wily bass are hooked, they deliberately swim through tangles of underwater obstacles in order to snag the line. Such an explanation is perhaps unduly elaborate. Most fish when alarmed attempt to return to a place where they feel safe, and for bass this seems to be a place well provided with underwater cover; once there, their frantic attempts to outrun the disturbing sensation of the hook in their jaws can be depended on to drape the line around just about every protuberance within easy range. (It is nice to know that it is highly unlikely that a fish can feel pain. Monster dairy bulls are routinely led about by means of rings through their noses, because pain is the penalty for non-compliance, but fish, with infinitely simpler nervous systems, cannot be "led by the nose" in this way.)

In the case of the **fly rod**, it is the **rod**, rather than the **reel**, which determines what the line must be like. Bearing in mind that the fly rod is designed to cast lures of practically no weight, it is evident that you can't simply wind a length of monofilament or braided synthetic onto a fly reel and expect it to work, because monofilament and braided synthetic simply don't weigh enough. What is more, fly line must also be considerably more tangle-resistant. One of the ways of filling its requirements both for weight and tangle-resistance is by increasing its bulk, so fly line tends to look like greenish or yellowish spaghetti.

Since fly rods were originally intended to catch surface-feeding trout, the earliest fly lines were designed to float if conscientiously greased, and were of uniform diameter all the way down their lengths. In the course of time, a number of fancy variations have been worked into the basic pattern. The three standard variables are: **shape, weight**, and **floatability**.

1. **Shape.** Most fly lines are (a) **level**–the same diameter throughout–(b) **double taper**–tapered at both ends, with the greatest diameter in the middle–and (c) **weight forward**–level for most of their lengths, with the forward portion double-tapered.

Here is the same data, expressed diagrammatically:

Level (L):

Fish
End

Fisherman
End

Double Taper (DT):

Fish
End

Fisherman
End

Weight Forward (WF);

Fish
End

Fisherman
End

Each of these types has certain advantages and disadvantages:

Level line is the least expensive, and, if you lose a foot or two of length to abrasion or underwater snags, it will not materially affect the rod's performance.

The extra weight amidships of the double-tapered line makes it possible to drop the fly at greater distances than those attainable with the level line, and at the same time insures that the part of the line closest to the fish, being of small diameter, will be relatively inconspicuous. If you lose the first few feet, thereby rendering the fish end unduly bulky, you can simply reverse the line fore to aft, without materially affecting the performance of the rod.

Weight-forward line is the easiest type of all to cast, but if you lose the first few feet, you have to get a new line. There are several kinds, each designed for a different use; for example, the "rocket taper" is designed to present small flies with great delicacy, while "bug taper" is designed to present cork or deer-hair bass bugs.

2. **Weight.** The weight of a fly line is normally based on the number of grains of weight for the first 30 feet of length, beginning at the fish end, but for convenience it is

normally quoted in numbers from 1 (light) to 12 (heavy). Bait-casting and fixed-spool rods can accommodate a wide range of lines of different pound-test strengths, but fly rods don't work that way: there is only one weight of line that is ideal for any particular fly rod, and any variations, either heavier or lighter, tend to impair the rod's performance, at least to some degree. (Graphite rods are considerably less exacting in this respect.) The very best way for an experienced fly fisherman to select the proper weight of line for a particular rod is to choose the line that "feels right" when worked with the rod; those less experienced will have to fall back on more indirect evidence. Most fly rods nowadays are marked with the weight of the line that normally goes with it, either right on the rod or in the literature accompanying it; since everybody's style of rod manipulation is a little different, the manufacturer's recommendations are not infallible, but will work most of the time for most people.

3. **Floatability.** You can get fly line that floats (labeled F), line that sinks (S), and line that floats most of its length but allows the front few feet to sink (ST, for "sinking tip").

Any properly-labeled fly line will bear a notation describing its characteristics in terms of all three of these variables, in the order given above. L 6 F is Level, No. 6 (fairly light), Floating; DT 8 S is Double Taper, No. 8 (medium), Sinking; WF 10 ST is Weight Forward, No. 10 (heavy), Sinking Tip, and so on.

In Chapter 1 we explored the process of choosing a rod and reel, or several rods and reels. The same process can be carried a step further: assuming the acquisition of a certain rod and reel, what would be a good, serviceable, general-purpose line to put on it?

In my opinion, the following table is as good as any:

Type of Rod	Line
BAIT-CASTING (about 6' long)	10-pound braided nylon or dacron
SPIN-CASTING (about 6½' or 7' long)	6-pound monofilament
SPINNING (about 7' long)	4-pound monofilament
FLY (about 8' long)	WF 8 F

Next question: Assuming the presence of a reel and its appropriate line, how do you get the line onto the reel?

Bait-casting reels. Braided synthetic usually comes in spools thoughtfully provided with holes to accommodate a pencil, a nail, or a length of doweling on which the spool can be made to revolve. Insert the doweling or what not through the hole, have a friend, child, or other captive relative hold the ends of the doweling, thread the end of the line through the level wind, tie it to the reel shaft (the reel shaft usually has a small hole drilled through it), and crank away until all the line is wound onto the reel: The project may be complicated somewhat by the fact

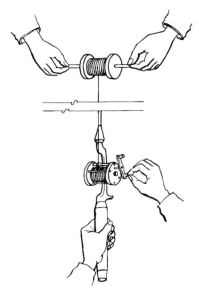

that a bait-casting reel when ready for use should be comfortably full–as full as you can get it without risk of impeding the free revolution of the spool; at the same time, the steel shaft of the reel is usually quite slender, about the diameter of a lead pencil, and hence, although you only

<hr>

Notes to the chart at left (1) Spin-casting rods tend to throw slightly heavier lures than spinning rods, or, putting it another way, have difficulty throwing lures as light as those thrown by spinning rods–hence the tendency toward a slightly shorter rod and a somewhat heavier line. (2) Again, a No. 8 fly line works with an 8-foot fly rod only if the rod is of medium flexibility–if it is stiffer or more limber, the weight will have to be adjusted accordingly.

need about 50 yards of line, the reel will probably hold 100 yards or more. This problem can be solved in any one of several ways:

1. You can increase the diameter of the shaft by means of a sleeve made of wood or cork (sometimes called a "mandrel") and then wind the line on top of the sleeve.

2. You can wind backing, a length of stronger but cheaper line, onto the shaft, tie on the braided synthetic, and wind it on top of the backing.

3. You can live recklessly and wind 100 yards or more of braided synthetic directly onto the shaft, realizing that the likelihood of using more than 50 yards of it will be slight.

About the same sort of procedure works for the monofilament that goes on **fixed-spool reels**. Most spinning reels are fitted with removable spools, so a fisherman with one spool on his reel and another in his pocket can easily switch from lighter to heavier lines, or vice-versa.

Both spin-casting and spinning reels should contain as much line as they can hold without interfering with the action of the reel. In the case of spinning reels, this will usually work out at about 1/16" from the rim.

The **fly-rod reel**, like any other reel, works best when it is as full as it can get without risk of jamming the mechanism. Because of the greater bulk of the line, and the lack of any special mechanism to assist neat line stowage, clearance should be greater than for monofilament–about 1/8".

Most fly reels are too deep to be filled up by line sold in its standard lengths (about 90 or 100 feet) and hence fly line is almost always wound on top of backing, usually braided synthetic. There is no point in being ladylike about it–you might as well use 20-pound test.

The trick is to wind a fly line of definite length onto a reel so that it will be comfortably full, with the line on top of the backing. This will require use of an additional reel, either another fly reel, a bait-casting reel, or simply a home-made contraption similar to those used by serious-minded kite-flyers:

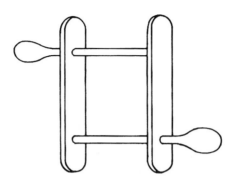

Procedure is as follows:

1. Tie the end of the fly line loosely to the reel, and wind on the line.

2. tie on the backing and wind on until the reel is full, ⅛" below the rim; cut off the synthetic. You now have the exact length of line and backing you want, but it is on backwards, with the line *under* the backing.

3. Unwind the backing by winding it onto your spare reel. Untie the backing from the line.

4. Unwind the line from the reel. Since it is designed to be kink-resistant, you don't have to wind it onto anything–drape it over a chair, or simply spread it out in coils on the floor. Untie it from the reel.

5. Tie the end of the backing onto the reel, and wind on. Since there is no level-wind mechanism, you should wind it on carefully, making sure that it is laid on smoothly.

6. Tie the end of the fly line to the end of the backing. (If it is a Weight Forward line, be sure you don't have it on backwards.) Crank it on, and your fly reel is ready for business.

3. Leader

It is possible to tie a hook or an artificial lure directly to a fishing line, but it is often useful to interpose a leader, a relatively short length of material that differs from the line in strength, diameter, or visibility. You might want to use a leader for one or several of the following reasons:

1. **To avoid loss of line.** If you used a leader of a pound-test rating less than that of the line, you could be fairly sure that if a fish managed to break loose, you would lose only the leader, and not the line as well. Although a serious matter for a commercial fisherman deploying long lines of gang hooks, this is not too important for most kinds of sport fishing.

2. **To prevent the fish from biting through the line.** Some fish are armed with sharp teeth or rasping mouth parts, and can bite or saw through some surprisingly tough materials, and so leaders of piano wire or steel cable are sometimes used.

3. **To reduce visibility of the line.** Some fish are by nature more suspicious than others. Monofilament is almost invisible in water, and hence a bait or lure attached to a line by a strand of monofilament looks more natural than one tied directly to a more easily visible line.

4. **To enable a fly-fisherman to present a fly to the fish as unobtrusively as possible.**

In view of the above, it would seem that the only time you don't need a leader is when fishing for toothless, dim-witted fish in murky water with a reel provided with lots of line and a slipping clutch. Actually, it depends partly on the size of lure used and the way it is manipulated. For example, if you were fishing for big bass with a fairly hefty plug, it is unlikely that your chances of success would be improved any by incorporating a nearly invisible leader, even if you were using clearly visible braided line–the size and motion of the plug seem to make the presence of the line less noticeable. However, if you were still-fishing with a worm, so that any fish in the vicinity could examine it at length, your chances of catching the same kind of bass would probably be considerably improved if there was a foot or so of less visible material between the bait and the end of the line.

For almost every kind of fishing, leader is simply a length of ordinary monofilament of a pound-test rating slightly lower than that of the line it is to be used with.

Almost, but not quite. Leader for fly fishing is a whole new ball game.

Remember that a fly rod was originally designed to deposit a fly on the water in such a way as to create the impression that the fly had fallen there naturally. To a trout, one of the least trusting of fish, even the thinnest fly line undoubtedly looks like the Atlantic Cable, so some sort of leader is indicated. Ordinary monofilament won't do—it's too limp, and if you tried to use it, the fly would go everywhere except where you wanted it to go. What is more, a length of special fly-line monofilament of a given pound-test strength won't do either—in order to work properly, the leader must taper down from the end of the line to the fly. This can be arranged in either of two ways:

1. **You can tie your own leader.** To do this, you will have to buy spools of special fly-line monofilament in graduated sizes (fly-line leader material is graded from 0-X (coarsest) to 7-X (finest), rather than in pound test), cut a short bit from each spool, and splice them together to make a tapered leader. The short bits can't be all of the same length, either—that would be too simple—they will have to be cut shorter or longer according to formulae computed by physicists using advanced mathematics and possibly witchcraft.

2. **You can buy a ready-made tapered leader**, with the mathematics already built into it. Although more expensive in the long run, it certainly saves a lot of fussing. Tapered leaders tend to come in standard lengths of 71/2, 9 and 12 feet, with different ranges of coarseness to fineness, but perhaps the commonest are those of 71/2 feet, ranging from 0-X to 4-X.

Even using a tapered leader does not completely eliminate the need for splicing. How fine the very end of the leader ought to be will depend on the size of fly you are using, so if you change from a smaller to a bigger fly, or vice-versa, you will have to make the appropriate adjustment. This is best done by means of a tippet, a length of special monofilament you tie onto the very end of your tapered line to adjust to the size of the particular fly you are using. You can get little spools of tippet material in all sizes from 1X to 7X.

One size too big or too small probably wouldn't hurt, but the best match-up of leader dimension to size of fly is:

Leader Dimension	Size of Fly
1-X	1 through 6
2-X	8
3-X	12
4-X	14
5-X	16
6-X	18 or 20
7-X	20 or 22

To recapitulate: The tapered leader is tied to the line, and the tippet is tied to the leader. As an absolute minimum, you should always have with you an extra spool of 4-X and 5-X.

Leader or tippet material sometimes develops kinks or curls; when this happens, it can usually be straightened out by pulling it through a fold of flexible rubber–a piece of inner-tube, for instance.

4. Knots

Just as, in the old spiritual, "the toe-bone is fastened to the ankle-bone, and the ankle-bone is fastened to the leg-bone," so also is the hook fastened to the leader, the leader to the line, the line to the reel, and the reel to the rod. The reel is fastened to the rod by means of any of several kinds of clamps, but all the other join-ups are knots.

There are two primary qualities that you are looking for in a knot. In the first place, you want a knot that will not come untied when subjected to strain. Anybody who goes fishing nowadays has to cope with nylon monofilament, and nylon really doesn't knot very willingly: because of its springiness and relatively hard surface–the very qualities that make it work well with spinning rigs–it takes a good knot to make it hold.

Secondly–perhaps equally important–you want a knot that will not unduly reduce the rated strength of the material used. Each fishing situation calls for a line of the appropriate strength rating–the number of pounds of tension the line can withstand without parting–and if you have chosen a fairly stout line to fish with, but have tied the lure to the line with a knot that kinks the line unduly, you may find to your dismay that if you have snagged an underwater weed, a four-pound tug on a ten-pound line may cause the line to break just at the point where you tied the knot, leaving your lure in the murky depths.

That standby of Boy-Scoutery, the **Bowline**, can be used whenever you need a rough-and-ready loop that won't slip–for example, when tying line to a reel shaft. Make a loop at the end of the line . . .

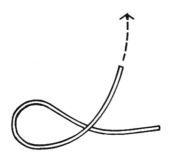

...pass the end of the line through the hole in the shaft...

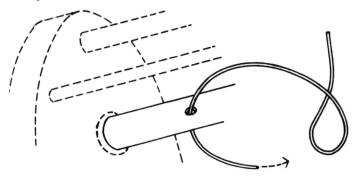

... pass the end of the line through the loop, entering from the rear ...

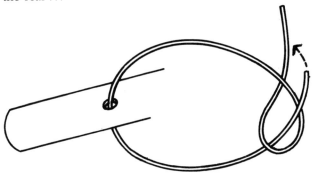

... around the back of the line . . .

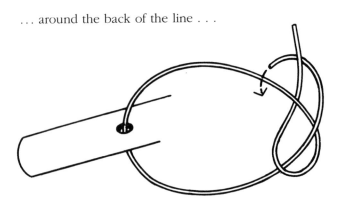

... and back through the loop again.

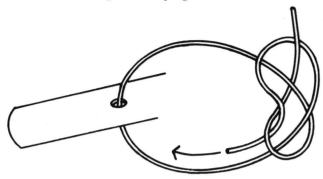

Pull tight.

If you want to tie a loop at the end of the line with minimum reduction in the pound-rated strength of the line, you can use an **End-Loop Knot**:

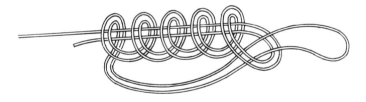

A good knot for tying together two lines of approximately equal diameter, or for tying fly-line tippets to the leader is the **Barrel Knot**:

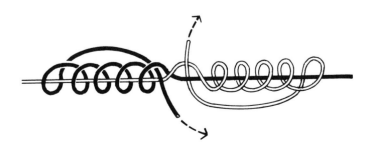

To provide a smooth and firm fastening between lines of unequal diameter, you can use a **Surgeon's Knot**, sometimes called the **Needle Knot**. It is especially useful for fastening leader to fly line. Pass the threaded needle through the core of the line and out the side . . .

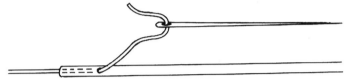

. . .wind the leader loosely around the line for five or six turns . . .

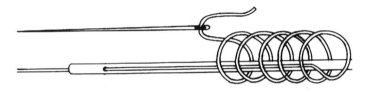

. . . and then pass the leader through the loops you have just made.

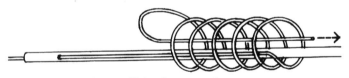

Pull tight and cut off the loose end.

If you want to replace a fly leader while on a fishing trip, and you don't have a needle with you, but you do have a ball-point pen, you can use a **Nail Knot** instead. It is called a nail knot because in its original form you used a big nail to hold the coils far enough apart so you could insinuate the leader past the nail and through the coils. However, it is much more convenient to use a two-inch length of small-bore tubing, like the plastic ink magazine in a ball-point pen, and shove the leader right through the tube. Wind the leader around both line and tube (you don't have to worry about keeping the coils especially loose) . . .

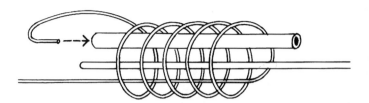

. . . and thread the leader through the tube.

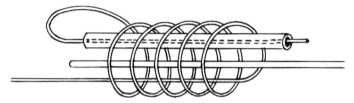

Remove the tube, pull tight, and cut off the loose end.

One of the ways of tying a leader to a hook is to use a **Turle Knot**. Pass the leader through the eye of the hook, make a loop, and take two turns around it . . .

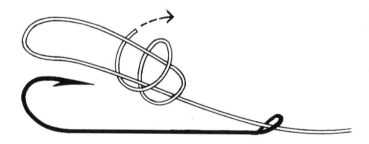

. . . pass the end of the leader through the first turn . . .

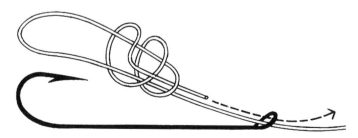

...and pass the end back through the eye of the hook.

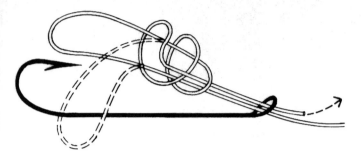

Flip the loop over the business end of the hook . . .

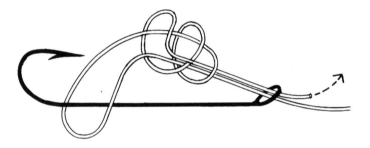

Pull tight, and cut off the loose end.

The turle doesn't work too well on dry flies, because the loops keep getting tangled in the hackle. For dry flies you can use the **Improved Clinch**, or **Blood Knot** instead. Pass the tippet through the eye of the fly, take five or six turns around the approach portion of the tippet, insert the end through the first turn . . .

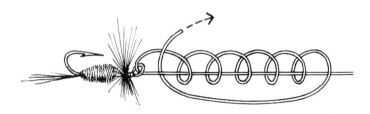

...and then pass the end through its outer bend.

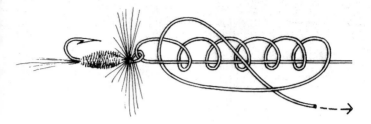

Pull tight and cut off the loose end.

Most bait fishermen used snelled hooks. A **Snelled Hook** is one that is knotted to a leader, formerly of gut but nowadays usually of monofilament, furnished with a loop, ready for fastening onto the end of the line. Nobody seems to know exactly where the word "snell" comes from, but it seems to have some connection (in Anglo-Saxon, Dutch, or Scandinavian) with the word for "quick." It may be that some antique fisherman, realizing that tying a hook to a line so as to produce a strong, inconspicuous join takes more time (and is harder to do when your fingers are numb with cold) than fastening two pieces of line together, hit onto the idea of tying hooks onto leaders in his spare time, so that when actually fishing, changing hooks was merely a matter of fastening line and leader together with a loop or simple knot. You can buy snelled hooks ready-made, but every fisherman ought to know how to tie his own.

To snell a hook, pass the end of the leader through the eye of the hook and take five or six turns around the shank ...

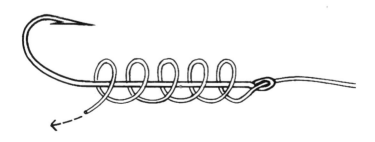

...tighten...

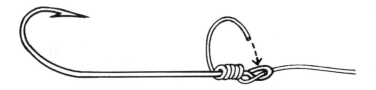

...pass the end of the leader through the first turn...

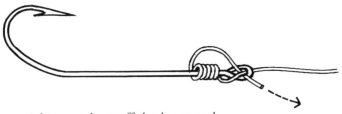

...tighten, and cut off the loose end.

The handiest way to fasten a snelled hook (or, for that matter, an artificial lure) to a line is by means of a **Snap Swivel**. Slip the bight of the bowline over the hook of the snap swivel.

...and close the snap.

However, if the kind of fishing you are going to be doing is the kind in which the fish is likely to be spooked by the glitter of metal, you can simply "birdseye" the loop of the line to the loop of the leader. Pass the loop of the leader through the loop of the line . . .

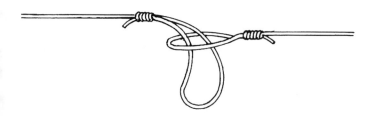

. . . pass the hook through the loop of its own leader . . .

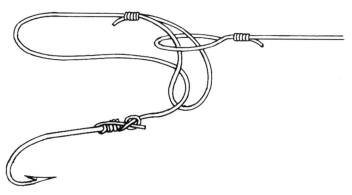

. . . and pull tight.

5. Hooks

There are many kinds of hooks, all with fancy names, and if you want to drive yourself crazy, you can spend many an hour trying to figure out the small ways in which the Aberdeen, Carlisle, Cincinnati, Kirby, Limerick, O'Shaughnessy, Pennell, Sproat, and a couple hundred others differ. Study of these various types may have been useful some years ago, when tempering of steel was less of an exact science than it is now, but the use of more precisely alloyed steel and controlled tempering have made the problem of exact hook shape less important. Personally, I like the Eagle Claw for most purposes–probably because it *looks* so efficient.

There is a rule of thumb whereby the efficiency of a hook can be estimated:

The most critical factor affecting the efficiency of a hook is its angle of penetration. It must be remembered that when a fisherman lifts his rod tip to set the hook, he is attempting to drive the barb into the tissues of the fish's mouth, and this will work only if the point of the hook is driven along an axis more or less parallel to the direction of his pull on the line. If you tie a hook to a line, and pull it through the water, the axis along which the hook is moving will pass through a point somewhere in the vicinity of the barb, the exact point depending on the dimensions and conformation of the hook.

If the hook is so made that its point is aimed along a line more or less parallel to this axis of line movement, the barb will act like a tiny spear . . .

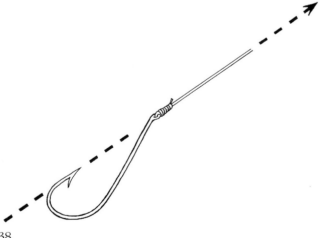

...but the wider the angle between the axis of aim and the axis of movement, the more inefficient the action of the hook will be–in practical terms, the more likely it will be that the barb, instead of imbedding itself in the fish's mouth tissues, will tear loose.

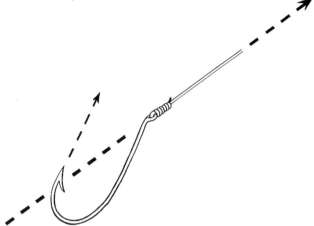

Almost any standard hook you buy will have good holding characteristics when new, but it frequently happens that a fisherman continues to fish with a hook that has been accidentally bent, unaware that he is attempting to operate with a hook that cannot possibly hold. Inspect your hook from time to time, especially after having pulled it loose from a snag, and if the axis-of-aim/axis-of-movement angle is excessive, throw it away.

So much for single hooks. There are also double and treble hooks.

Treble hooks are widely used on artificial lures, at least partly because there is no telling from which angle the fish is going to attack. Treble hooks can also be an awful pain in the neck, especially when using bottom-bumping lures that keep getting hung up every ten seconds. In such a case, you can replace the treble with a double hook, arranged so that both points turn upward, or you can simply cut off the downward-pointing shank of the triple hook. This may be a little harder to do than it appears at first glance.

If you fasten a treble hook to the end of the line, and drag the line so the hook bumps along the bottom, there is no telling which of the three arms of the hook is going to point downward, and so the likelihood of getting hung up on the bottom with this kind of arrangement will range from fair to excellent, depending on the type of bottom (rocky, sandy, or what not), and the presence or absence of snaggable materials in the water. However, if the treble hook is connected to a lure which, by virtue of its shape, maintains its top surface up and its bottom surface down, you can rig the treble hook so that one of the three arms points directly downward, and then snip off the down-ward-pointing arm, with its outstandingly snaggable barb, using a pair of cutting pliers.

For example, a wobbling spoon always rides in the water with the concave side up. The spoon itself is there-fore always horizontal to the bottom. A split ring thread-ed through a hole in the aft end of the spoon will there-fore be vertical, and the eyelet of a treble hook threaded through the split ring will, like the spoon itself, be hori-zontal.

Here comes the tricky part: *it is therefore possible to rig the treble hook two ways–one arm up, and two arms down* [wrong], *or one arm down and two arms diagonally up* [right]. Rig it with one arm down and two arms diagonal-ly up, cut off the downward arm, and the spoon, being now provided with a hook whose two remaining arms curve gently away from the bottom, will be relatively snag-free:

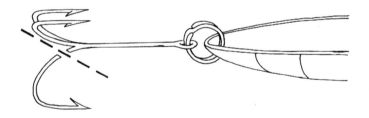

6. Attractors

If you have a rod, a reel, a line, and possibly a leader, all that remains is to put something on the end of it that will attract fish.

Fish, like people, seem to have equivalents to what used to be classified as the five senses: Seeing, Hearing, Feeling, Tasting, and Smelling. Some pessimists would add that they are also skilled in Extra-Sensory Perception, mind-reading, and Black Magic, but we have no positive evidence of this.

1. *Seeing*. The visual acuity of fish seems to vary all the way from Very Sharp to Medium Poor, depending on the breed.

If you see a trout fisherman crawling on his hands and knees through the bushes bordering a small stream, it is probably not because he has lost a contact lens, but because he knows that if he stands up too close to the stream, any trout in that particular pool will see him and be frightened off. It is therefore evident that trout can see not only what is going on in the water, but to a degree what is going on above it as well.

Trout are not the only fish with good eyesight. Some years ago, when in Washington State, I used to frequent a lake near where I lived, and fish for crappie with tiny spoons. More than once, while so doing, they wouldn't really start biting until it got so dark that it was hard to believe that they could possibly see the lure.

On the other hand, since it is possible to catch catfish at midnight, deep down in the channel of the murkiest possible river, it seems likely that, regardless of whether a catfish's eyesight is particularly good or not, he doesn't need it to feed with. This hypothesis is borne out by the fact that catfish are provided with whisker-like barbels, with which they examine the bottom by what seems to be feel, and by the fact that each veteran catfish angler seems to have his own private formula for catfish bait, invariably involving cheese, chicken-blood, or other strongly-flavored ingredients, implying that a catfish can home in on it by odor, about as accurately as a cat can home in on the odor of fresh liver.

2. *Hearing*. There are lures that vibrate or buzz, and it is possible that the sound, as distinct from the sight, of an insect which has fallen into the water and is struggling to get out is attractive to fish, but the technique of using noises to attract fish doesn't seem to be given much

emphasis. Instead of worrying about noises likely to attract fish, the fisherman would be well advised to avoid the noises that scare fish away. It should be obvious by now that the old idea that serious fishing and conversation don't mix "because it scares the fish" is absurd, doubtless the invention of some antisocial curmudgeon who hated idle chatter. The kind of noises that really do scare fish away are the short, sharp vibrations that are readily transmitted through the ground or a boat to the water–clumping heavily along the bank, shipping oars with more abandon than precision, kicking the bait bucket, and the like. I have known people who will spend most of their fishing time rattling through a tin tacklebox with the sound of a suit of armor falling downstairs (every rattle faithfully transmitted to the water via the bottom of the boat) and then wonder why "they aren't biting."

Incidentally, as you may have noticed, fish don't have ears. They hear by means of what is known as the "lateral line," a string of nerve endings distributed along two lines, one on each side, between gills and tail, about half way between the dorsal fin and the belly. In many fish, the lateral line is clearly visible.

3. *Feeling.* Sturgeon normally feed by cruising an inch or so off the bottom, their fleshy whiskers twiddling along the pebbles, and when the whiskers contact something that might be edible, a conical tube where their mouths should be shoots out and sucks in whatever it is, so it is possible that sturgeon feed more or less by feel. It is also possible that taste and smell are also involved–those whiskers are pretty special.

One point at which feel becomes critical is when a fish chomps down on an artificial fly–instead of a nice squuddy mass of protein, he gets a mouthful of wire and bristles. This is why fly-fishing fanatics insist that when a trout strikes at a dry fly, you should lift the tip of the rod *at once*, before the trout realizes how shabbily he has been treated.

4. *Tasting and Smelling.* These ought to be considered together, because they keep getting confused, even by human beings. The only human taste sensations there are are sweet, sour, salt, and bitter; everything else–strawberry, vanilla, coffee, Romanee-Conti–is odor.

The sensitivity of sharks to taste/odor is notorious: a shark can detect the presence of extremely small quantities of blood in the water, and follow a blood trail, possibly several miles long, just as precisely as a bloodhound can follow the trail of a lost child.

The sense of taste/odor that some fish have can also go beyond the simple function of homing in on something edible, as an experiment with catfish has demonstrated. A researcher maintained several catfish, each in its own tank. At the bottom of each tank was a piece of tile in the shape of half a cylinder, forming a tunnel. The fish were fed by hand, and got accustomed to people moving about in the room where the tanks were kept. One day, the researcher deliberately frightened one of these catfish, which, with every appearance of alarm, darted away and hid in its tunnel. The researcher then dipped out some of the water from its tank, and dumped it into the tank inhabited by a second catfish. The second catfish, which had been serenely cruising up and down, at peace with the world, immediately darted off and, like the first, hid in its tunnel. Apparently, the odor of fear given off by the first catfish was enough to communicate the same kind of alarm to the second.

All in all, most fishermen most of the time seem to use fish attractors that appeal to sight, to taste/smell, or both. Typical of attractors that appeal primarily (or even exclusively) to sight are artificial lures; typical of those that appeal primarily to taste/smell are baits; typical of attractors that appeal to both are combinations of bait and artificial lures.

7. Bait

A bait can be defined as anything that a fish would normally be willing to eat, used to induce that fish to bite. They are sometimes called "natural baits," to distinguish them from artificial lures, but this is a little misleading. There are all sorts of baits that are not at all part of the normal environment of the fish which is supposed to be conned into biting on them: carp will readily take doughballs; rainbow trout seem to be fond of corn niblets (although some people seem to feel it is bad for them); almost any kind of fish will happily gobble up salmon eggs, even though the fish who do the gobbling live in waters that salmon could not possibly tolerate. It probably works with fish as it does with people: an American diplomat in Saudi Arabia could conceivably be agreeably stimulated by the appetising odor of the dinner being served, and consume it with gusto, without knowing (or caring) that it is roast camel.

Technically, a **minnow** is any member of the fish family *Cyprinidae*, of which there are about 300 kinds in the United States alone. (The carp is a member of the *Cyprinidae*, so the next time you see an angler proudly exhibiting a 20-pound carp, you can with perfect accuracy say, "Nice minnow you have there.") However, to a fisherman, a minnow is just about any small fish that can be used live for bait.

One of the things about using a live minnow for bait is that the minnow does most of the work for you. There he is, desperately trying to get away, and, if in good shape, kicking up quite a fuss doing it. Fish have never appreciated the moral beauty of refraining from taking advantage of a fellow fish when he is down, and the very fact that the minnow is in trouble makes it all the more attractive to bigger fish–they have no doubt learned that the bigger fuss a small creature makes in the water, the more easily he can be caught and eaten.

You can buy live minnows or you can catch your own. I remember stopping by a bait stand in Louisiana to pick up some minnows. The proprietor was of course desirous of delivering his livestock to the customer alive and in good shape, so he fed them in moderation, kept the water in the tanks cool, and maintained aerators–little pumps that kept air bubbling through the water–so the minnows would have plenty of oxygen. Well, I made off with my tigers. As long as they remained in their carton of still-cool (and heavily-oxygenated) water, they kept darting about briskly, but as soon as I fastened one of them to a hook and dropped him into the bayou, he immediately collapsed, gulping feebly. And no wonder. Louisiana bayous in the summertime are low in oxygen, and have the temperature (and sometimes the consistency) of warm soup; the sudden contrast was just too much. If you came in from an afternoon of skiing, and immediately plunged into a hermetically-sealed sauna, you wouldn't be so brisk either.

One way of heading off collapse of this kind, or at least postponing it for a while, is to change the water in the minnow bucket gradually. Dip out a cup of water from the bucket, and replace it with water from the lake or stream you are fishing; wait a while, and repeat the process; keep this up long enough, and eventually the water in the bucket will be pretty much like the water you want to fish in.

Incidentally, the kind of bait bucket to use is either one made of permeable plastic, or a metal one with a plastic liner. In some mysterious way, the permeable plastic allows air to enter the water where the fish are, and to a degree compensate for the loss of oxygen that invariably takes place when fish are confined in a small container for any length of time. The warmer the day, the faster the rate at which deoxygenation takes place.

Of course, if you get the minnows from the very same water you are fishing, the process of maintaining them in an athletic frame of mind is simplified somewhat.

Minnows can be caught in several ways. Two people, at opposite ends of a piece of fine-mesh netting about 3' X 8', the ends tacked to skinny fence-posts to keep the material taut, can, by sweeping a stretch of water in which minnows have been observed, starting in deeper water and driving toward shallower water, round up minnows, and possibly a few frogs and crayfish as well.

Another method is to use a sweep net. Fortunately, most minnows prefer relatively shallow water, so the engineering involved does not have to be elaborate.

Proceed as follows:

1. Procure a square of fine mesh netting, about 3' X 3', or as large as you think you can conveniently handle.

2. Fasten to a lightweight, non-bulky frame–two stout rods fastened together crosswise will do it.

3. Suspend this apparatus from a harness consisting of four cords of equal length joining the ends of the frame to another piece of cord.

4. Suspend apparatus and harness from a stout pole:

5. Lower the net to the bottom and bait with doughballs or other bait.

6. When minnows have come to investigate the bait, hoist away. If you hoist rapidly enough, the netting will sag enough to nudge the minnows toward the center of the net. It is generally a good idea to have a two-man recovery team—one hoisting and the other grabbing minnows and dropping them into the bait bucket—otherwise you'll lose a lot of minnows.

Still another method is to use a minnow trap. You can buy minnow traps of wire or glass, or you can make your own. Minnow traps usually consist of a cone-shaped passage leading to an inner chamber; the cone guides the minnow into the chamber, but, once inside, he has difficulty finding the small end of the cone, and hence cannot get out again.

Minnow traps work best if placed so as to intercept normal minnow traffic, as in the middle of a small stream flowing into a lake. So placed they are likely to work just about as well if positioned to intercept upstream as down-stream traffic.

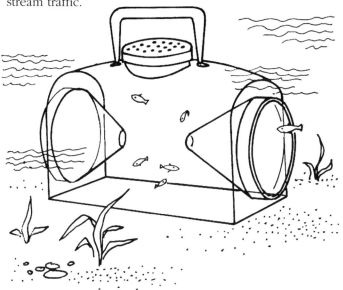

Like sweep nets, they are usually baited with dough-balls, crumbs, or other provender likely to appeal to small fish.

There are fancy ways of putting minnows on hooks, but any way that holds the minnow securely without killing him is a good way. The commonest methods are through the muscle just ahead of the dorsal, or back, fin (being careful not to puncture the spine) or through the lips–in the upper and out the lower. How the minnow avoids suffocating with a hook through his lips I don't know, but he does. If the barb shows, don't worry about it–contrary to persistent folklore, fish don't seem to draw any sinister conclusions from a protruding barb. (This applies not only to minnows but also to anything else you put on a hook.)

Frogs, especially small ones, make excellent bait for large, movement-motivated fish like bass or pike. They are best hunted at night–again, this is best done as a two-man operation. As one slowly eases a canoe or rowboat along frog-rich waters (edges of swamps or small streams), the other mans a flashlight. Frogs, like most amphibians, avoid both deep water and really dry land, so the place to look for them is right along the shoreline or lolling in the water with their noses sticking out. During the day they can see you coming, but at night the frog can't see anything but the light shining in his face, so he can be scooped up with a small hand net and dumped into a damp sack. (If you are *very* fast, you can catch him by hand.)

You can hook frogs through the lips, like minnows, but not through the back–too bony. Some authorities hook them through the muscle of a hind leg, which results in a rather lively bait.

The classic method of catching **crayfish** is by means of a piece of meat hung on a stick-and-string arrangement, and a small net–a home-made one will do.

1. Let the meat fall to the bottom.

2. When the crayfish starts working on the bait, *slowly* raise the rod until bait and crayfish are just under the surface of the water. The crayfish will object to the bait rising, but won't want to let go, either.

3. Some authorities insist on lifting the meat and crayfish clear of the water, but you probably will lose fewer crayfish if you insinuate the dipnet under the crayfish while he is still in the water, and then scoop briskly upward.

Crayfish are best hooked through their back-armor; the hook goes in at the neck-joint and comes out farther down the back.

There are a number of underwater insects, especially those that are found under stones in streams, that make good bait. They seem to sort themselves out into two groups–the agile and the less agile.

Typical of the first group is the **hellgrammite**, the larval form of the dobson fly, which looks like a blackish or brownish centipede. To catch hellgrammites, overturn stones, watch for movement, and pounce. (Careful–they nip.) Hellgrammites (and just about any other hard-shelled insect, for that matter) are hooked much like cray-fish–the hook goes in at the back of the neck and emerges a little farther down the back. The idea is to slip the bend of the hook under just enough armor-plate to insure that the insect will remain securely attached, thus avoiding the possibility of impaling him so deeply that he will die, depriving you of the advantages of a lively bait.

Typical of the second group is the **caddis worm**, the larval form of the mayfly or caddis fly. These are small grubs encased in cocoons, made of sand, gravel, or rub-bish of any kind. Being slow-moving, they are easier to catch than hellgrammites, and since you aren't going to get any action out of them anyway, simply impale them on the hook. Fish, including trout, eat them cocoon and all, so you can either shuck off the cocoon or fish with them as is.

Grasshoppers make good bait. They tend to spend the night clinging to grain-stems, coarse grass, or tall weeds, and so the time to gather them is as early in the morning as it is light enough to see them by: the com-bination of lower temperature, darkness, and possibly dampness (from dew) makes them torpid and slow-moving. The hardest thing about using grasshoppers is preventing them from escaping while taking them out of the box you have stored them in. To prepare an escape-proof bait box:

1. Paste a small cardboard box, punched full of small air-holes, completely closed with masking tape.

2. At one end, cut a slit along an edge, so that by squeezing the sides of the box, you can cause the slit to gape just enough so that you can insert a grasshopper head first. As soon as the grasshopper falls inside the box, relax pressure on the sides, and the slit will close.

At the other end of the box, cut off a corner just big enough to allow one grasshopper to squeeze through at a time, and close it off temporarily with a tab of masking tape. Whenever you need a grasshopper, tip the box over on its side and peel back the tab. The grasshoppers inside the box will crawl toward the light, looking for an exit. As soon as one of them wiggles through far enough to grab, grab him.

Crickets work pretty much like grasshoppers, except that they are easier to catch. They can be found under stones or in piles of hay or other loose material, or they can be flushed out of the grass by lawn-mowers.

The life cycle of both crickets and grasshoppers is tied to the springtime emergence of young from eggs laid the previous fall, so you usually don't find big ones until late summer or early fall.

In the United States, when a businessman describes the state of his business by saying, "I might as well have dug me a can of worms and gone fishing," we know exactly what he means.

In France, there is an expression which means just about the same thing, but is worded a little differently. The French version is, "I might as well have got me a supply of *asticots* and gone fishing."

What is an *asticot?*

The **asticot** is, without doubt, the most easily-procured and universally-ignored live bait in the United States. Moreover, most fish are crazy about them. To get some, all you have to do is tie a string to a piece of raw meat and suspend it in the warm sun over some sort of container. In a very short time, flies will appear and lay eggs on it, and the eggs will eventually hatch out into grubs. The grubs will happily crawl in and out and round about on the piece of meat, feeding as they go, and getting fatter all the time. Since they cannot climb up the string, most of them eventually fall into the container you have thoughtfully provided for them. *Asticot*-fanciers of my acquaintance recommend that the container be filled with bran, to prevent the grubs from being baked onto the container by the sun; since bran is a relatively scarce commodity in most households, other light, loose, dry materials, like sawdust, may be substituted. I have never tried oatmeal, but I don't see why it wouldn't work.

If the members of your family have a tendency toward squeamishness, locate your *asticot*-farm at some distance from the house.

Your knowledge of the habit flies have of laying their eggs on raw meat can also be used to transform a good fishing spot into a better one. If you happen to find a small dead animal–a mouse or a chipmunk, for example– near a fishing spot you frequent, it can do no harm to suspend it over the water on a string. Sooner or later, flies will lay eggs on it; the eggs will hatch; and the larvae will start falling into the water. If there are any fish in the vicinity, it will not take long before they converge on the spot to share the bounteous harvest, and they will normally hang about as long as the golden flow lasts–perhaps even a few days longer.

If the *asticot* is large and the hook small, you may fish with one at a time; with a bigger hook, it is probably better to string on three or four, to make up a more tempting package.

So much for *asticots*. Now for **worms**.

Although most Americans know that earthworms make good bait, a great many Americans apparently do not know how to keep them in fighting trim. The legendary tomato can is no good–an hour or so of stewing in its hot, airless depths is enough to reduce the most athletic and pugnacious worm to a lifeless mass of jelly. I use a plastic container with a tight-fitting lid that once held calves' liver. Both the lid and the bottom have been punched full of medium-sized holes, to insure a reasonable draft, partly to provide oxygen, and partly to keep the worms cool by water evaporation.

Whenever a fishing expedition involving worms is imminent, I half-fill the container with worms and some of the earth they were found in, insert a wad of damp grass, and pop in the lid. I store the container upside-down in the shade, blocking it up on something so that air can enter from below and circulate freely. Worms confined in limited quantities of earth seem to work their way downward, no doubt an instinct designed to get them away from both light and excessive dryness, so by the time I get around to using a worm, I turn the container right-side-up, take off the lid, and usually find most of the worms conveniently available, snuggled in the space between the dirt and the grass.

Worms stored like this have been known to maintain reasonable muscle-tone for a week or so–longer if care is taken that they don't dry out. It is a minor paradox of nature that although worms can live in very soggy ground, they drown fairly easily. For this reason, if you find your worm supply drying out, rather than sloshing it with water, it is better to replace some of the dried-out dirt with moist (not wet) dirt and re-dampen the wad of grass.

There are all sorts of ways to procure worms: you can shock them out of the ground with electric current; you can drown them out by inundating your lawn (or simply waiting for it to rain); you can raise them in boxes, feeding them with nourishing mixtures, almost invariably including corn meal and, for some reason, coffee grounds. You can even buy domestic worms raised for sale, doubtless paying the highest price per pound ever paid for livestock, regardless of type. However, if your requirements are not extreme, and you have access to a patch of well-shaded soil that isn't being used for anything else, you may be able to make do with the wild article.

In looking for them, it is a good idea to bear in mind that worms are not too fussy about in what kind of environment they find themselves, so long as it is moist, cool, and dark enough, not actually poisonous or corrosive, and provided with suitable nourishment. Awareness of this principle can save you a lot of digging. About fifty yards uphill from my house is a moist place strewn with rocks, shaded by big maple trees. The mixture of mud and rotting leaves is all the worms need to live on and in, so for at least a part of the fishing season, gathering worms for me consists simply of tipping up rocks and removing worms from under them.

If you don't have a convenient worm settlement nearby, a number of bricks laid on the ground on the shady side of the house, preferably under a hose outlet, or where rainwater drips from the eaves, could produce gratifying yields. Another possibility: a shady spot that can be induced to grow grass, either naturally damp or sprinkled from time to time, can be transformed into a reliable wormery. Dig up about a dozen sods, about as big as you can conveniently lift with the hands, and immediately replace them. In a few days, there ought to be a sizeable assemblage of worms just under the sods. Apparently what happens is that the worms, who, in common with other living creatures, do not care to work any harder than necessary, find the loose soil between the sods and the ground easier to crawl through and get food and oxygen from than dirt in its natural state, and hence tend to congregate there.

A worm has an advantage over an *asticot* in that, whereas the *asticot's* shape does not conduce to free movement once it is impaled on a hook, the worm, if properly impaled, adds movement to the basic attractants of visibility and taste/odor. For most purposes, pass the barb of the hook through the worm at two, three, or four places (depending on the length of the worm), leaving loops and ends to writhe and coil freely. Rather than impaling the worm sidewise through the body . . .

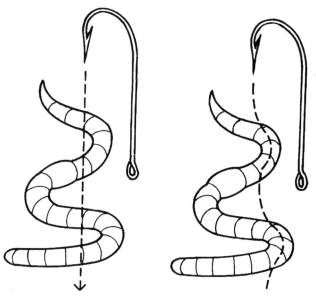

. . . it is better to pass the barb/in one side, through the body for a short distance, and out the same side the hook went in.

If you impale the worm sidewise through the body, you will have punched one hole more than necessary through the ring of muscle at the point of penetration, thus considerably increasing the likelihood of the worm breaking off (or being pulled off) the hook at this point.

Salmon eggs are used a lot on the West Coast, mostly for catching rainbow and cutthroat trout. Since mature salmon normally venture into fresh water only during the spawning season, and are very choosy about which particular stream they venture into, most people who use salmon eggs have to depend on commercial sources, like sporting-goods stores, as a source of supply. They (the salmon eggs, not the people) come in jars, either natural (orangey-red) or one of several fluorescent colors. They are fished either one at a time, on tiny hooks that are almost completely concealed within the egg, or in gobs held together in little cheesecloth bags.

If you open up a fish (in the spring for most breeds; in the fall for some) and find in the rearmost end of the body cavity two elongated masses of what looks like small-bore tapioca, the fish is a female and the masses are masses of roe.

There is no reason why the roe of fish other than salmon cannot be used as bait–salmon eggs, being sizeable, are simply more convenient–but any fish eggs big enough to be held together by the same kind of makeshift cheesecloth bag used for salmon eggs should work about as well.

It may come as something of a surprise that certain sizeable fish, like carp and mullet, normally feed on microscopic forms of plant and animal life. There is no point in trying to entice them with live bait or artificial lures–they just aren't interested–but they can sometimes be tempted with **doughballs**.

One way to make doughballs is as follows:

1. Put about half a cup of flour onto a big plate.

2. Add water a little at a time, stirring in flour until you have a modest wad of stiff dough. Go easy on the water, otherwise you will have more doughballs than you and ten other people will know what to do with.

3. If you keep turning and squeezing the mass long enough, adding more flour, if necessary, it will get unsticky enough so you can handle it with your fingers.

4. When it does, roll it into a long cylinder perhaps half an inch in diameter.

5. Cut off pieces of dough about half an inch long, roll them between your palms to produce a ball, and drop them into briskly-boiling water. The resulting dumplings will sink to the bottom of the pot, stay there until they are half-cooked, and then rise to the top. (Don't put in too many at one time, or they'll stick together. As many as will float without crowding is about enough.)

6. You can take them out as soon as they float, or you can let them boil another five or ten minutes just for luck. When you take them out, set them aside to cool.

7. If you let them stand too long, they will get too hard; if you don't let them stand at all, they will be too sticky for comfort. If you leave them alone for a few hours or overnight, they ought to be about right.

8. Store them in a container with a tightly-fitting lid.

The above is the least-common-denominator recipe; doughball fanciers frequently add various spices, flavorings, or other substances they imagine add appeal to the basic material. For example, if instead of water you used the liquid canned shrimp comes packed in, you would presumably add a temptingly fishy flavor to the resulting doughballs.

Bait for sea fish is a little special, partly because the supplies conveniently and abundantly available are different, but mostly because the environment is different. In the ocean, where killer whales, seals, sharks, swordfish, bluefish, tuna, and many other kinds of oversized non-vegetarians spend a good deal of their time dismembering and devouring various forms of vertebrate and invertebrate life, there are also many other breeds, large and small, that have no compunction about polishing off the left-overs, and so **cut bait**, chunks of just about any kind of natural protein–fish, shrimp, clams, squid–are widely used. You can get several varieties of **marine worms**, too–sandworms and bloodworms, with impressive-looking mouth parts. As a matter of fact, along the Maine coast, the prospects for a good sandworm year are just as seriously discussed as the prospects for a good lobster year.

One of the easiest shellfish to gather are **mussels**–the small blackish-purplish ones. On Vancouver Island, the tides are so high that most docks are made to float, restrained only by being loosely linked to long pilings; when the tide is out, you can pick them off the pilings without even getting your feet wet. It would seem reasonable to suppose that a shellfish so abundant and so easily gathered can't be good for anything, but this isn't so. They are not only good for bait, but are also fit for human consumption.

Until recently, they were not much eaten in the United States, but my Washington sources inform me that nowadays there is despair in the hearts of patrons of the seafood restaurants along Maine Street when they are informed that the supply of mussels has run out.

Mussels are pretty soft-bodied; if you find they come off the hook too easily, you can enclose them in cheesecloth, as with salmon eggs.

8. Artificial Lures

An artificial lure is an assemblage of wood, plastic, metal, rubber, fur, feathers, and other normally inedible substances, designed to induce fish to strike at it. Many artificial lures are obviously designed to masquerade as fish, frogs, mice, or other living creatures; others resemble nothing else on earth.

There are so many artificial lures on the market, with more coming along all the time, that it is just about impossible to list them all, much less describe them. Fortunately, it isn't necessary to do so. The number of ways artificial lures can be put together and manipulated to intrigue fish are limited, and hence most artificial lures tend to fall into a few well known categories.

A **plug** is a solid chunk of something, usually wood or plastic, designed to move through, or on top of, the water in a way calculated to arouse a fish's interest. A great many of them are so made as to produce a wobbling action as the plug is pulled through the water, either by scooping out the front end,

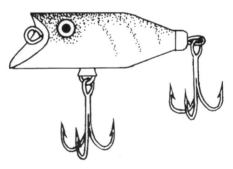

or by attaching a shaped metal tab.

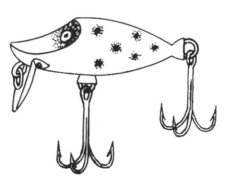

Others, especially floating plugs, are provided with propellers that churn the water and may or may not suggest to bigger fish the frantic efforts of a minnow with a dangerously overinflated swim bladder to escape to deeper water.

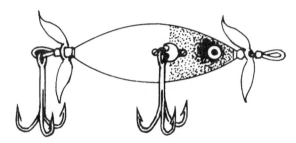

There is a kind of contraption that looks something like a plug but works on a totally different principle. Somebody once said that to an engineer the difference between an automobile and a horse and wagon is primarily a matter of how the power is applied: for the car, the fact that the wheels go around makes the car move; for the horse and wagon, the fact that the wagon moves makes the wheels go around. Well, a real fish wiggles his tail in order to move forward; this particular type of contraption, which we could arbitrarily call a **flipper**, moves forward in order to wiggle its tail. A more or less fish-shaped body is molded to a sheet of plastic in such a way as to set up a fairly fish-like vibration in the tail end when the lure is pulled through the water.

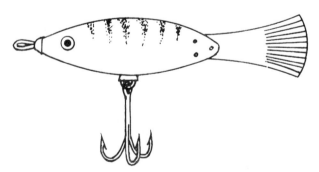

The term "spinner," when used to designate a type of artificial lure, is a little confusing. In this sense, a **spinner** has nothing to do with spinning reels, being merely an arrangement whereby movement through the water induces one or more blades to revolve around a central axis. The blade can be a propeller, or it can be a more or less spoon- or bowl-shaped blade. It can be made to revolve around a fixed shaft ...

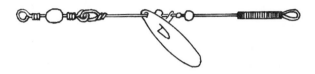

... or loosely linked to a pair of swivels.

Those swivels aren't there just for decoration—the action of the spinner tends to twist the line, and the swivel reduces (but does not eliminate) the twist. The easiest way to straighten out a twisted line is by taking off the lure and letting the line trail behind a moving boat, alternately letting out and cranking in the line. (As you retrieve, keep mild tension on the line by gently squeezing it with one hand while cranking with the other. If you don't the line may wind onto the reel so loosely as to get tangled in its own coils.) The next-best way to straighten out a twisted line is to lay it out on a lawn, again with nothing attached to it, and to crank it in again. Repeat several times.

A **spoon** is an artifact, usually (but not always) shaped more or less like the bowl of an ordinary spoon, which wobbles when drawn through the water. It can be of shiny metal, or painted in various colors and patterns. Hooks are attached to the spoon either rigidly,

or flexibly.

Rigid-hook spoons sometimes have strips of pork rind impaled on their hooks; flexible-hook spoons are sometimes festooned with tufts of feathers or hair.

Spoons normally don't twist the line unless retrieved too fast, in which case they will not only twist the line, but fail to catch fish. On the other hand, if you retrieve them too slowly, they won't wobble properly, and will also fail to catch fish.

Rubber worms come in several colors–purple was Very Big a while back–and are sometimes embellished with small spinners or hula skirts of hair or rubber.

They are usually fished by being pulled through the water with a series of short jerks. Fished this way, they don't resemble worms in the least, especially when provided with ballet skirts and flashers, but the fish either don't know this or don't care.

A **jig** is a mass of metal or other heavy material incorporating one or more hooks. Jigs are usually tubular or spindle-shaped, are of various colors and patterns, and are sometimes provided with tufts of feathers, hair, and what not.

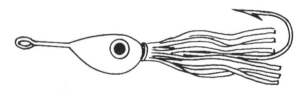

They can be fished in several ways, but the original idea (possibly dreamed up by aboriginal Eskimos) was to cut a hole in the ice, sit down next to it, let down the jig until it hits the bottom, and then keep bouncing it on the bottom until a fish, consumed by curiosity, strikes at it and gets hooked.

A **popper** is pretty much a dish-faced or flat-faced miniature floating plug, fished in a different way. Instead of being pulled through, or along the surface of, the water, it is moved along the surface in a series of short jerks, rather like a surface version of the rubber worm. Since it is a surface lure, it is sometimes provided with short lengths of rubber-band material, suggesting the legs of an insect or other small invertebrate.

It ought to be pretty obvious by now that explanations having to do with fly fishing tend to be longer and more complicated than explanations having to do with any other kind of fishing. The main thing about a **fly** is that it is usually anywhere between pretty small and quite tiny, and weighs close to nothing. (**Salmon flies**, a special breed, can be bigger.) For this reason, it is simply a hook onto which are wound, coiled, or otherwise fastened yarn, hair, fur, feathers (mostly feathers), strips of metal foil, or other improbable materials. Flies, like plugs, are sometimes intended to simulate living creatures–some of the earliest ones imitated specific insects in the minutest detail–but, somewhere along the way, some experimentally-minded individual found out that fish will strike at flies bearing no resemblance, in either color, shape, or pattern, to anything alive, or, for that matter, extinct, and so some are made that way.

The terminology used by fly fishermen is rather mysterious until you get to know the basic life cycle of the insects that artificial flies were originally designed to imitate. There is a class of insects, the *Ephemeridae*, comprising a number of species, of various shapes and colors. They are normally found in or near cool, highly-oxygenated water, the same kind of environment that favors trout, and trout eat them with what seems like gusto in all stages of their life cycle. The larval stage of these insects, the **nymph**, swims or crawls on the bottom, either as is or encased in a little protective tube made of pebbles, sticks, or rubbish. When it is due to mature, it swims to the surface, molts, emerges as a winged **dun**, and flies to shore. Once on shore, it molts again and becomes a **spinner**. (It is by now evident that (a) a spinning reel is a kind of reel; (b) a spinner is a kind of artificial lure, having nothing in particular to do with a spinning reel; and (c) a spinner is also the final stage in the life of a certain kind of insect, having nothing in particular to do with either spinning reels or artificial lures.) The female spinner mates, returns to the water, and deposits her eggs, which sink to the bottom, eventually hatch out as nymphs, and start the cycle all over again. After mating, both male and female versions of the insect, now known as **spents**, die, and a good many of them fall into the water.

Now then. A **wet fly** is designed to sink in the water, in imitation of a nymph. If it has wings at all, they will be folded against the body.

A **dry fly** is one designed to float. If its wings stick up in the air, either straight

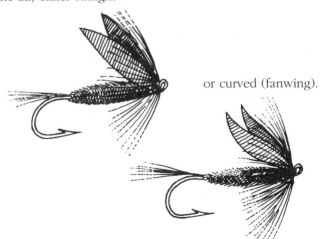

or curved (fanwing).

It is in imitation of a dun or spinner; if the wings are at right angles to the body, it is in imitation of a spent.

There is also a kind of dry fly known as a **bivisible**; as the name implies, it is in two colors, light and dark, and it isn't made in imitation of anything.

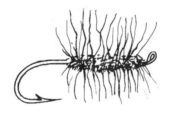

Dry-fly technique normally requires that the fisherman raise the tip of his rod the moment he sees the fly disappear (presumably sucked under by a trout) and the two-toned bivisible insures that he can keep the fly in view; the light part will show up against the dark water, and the dark part will show up against white water.

A **spider** is actually made in imitation of just about any land insect that accidentally falls in the water. It is made like an ordinary dry fly, except that it has neither wings nor tail.

A **deer-hair fly** is, naturally enough, made of deer hair. Deer hair is hollow, and hence this type of fly is exceptionally buoyant.

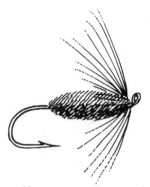

A **streamer fly** is one with extra-long wings that trail behind the body. When in the water, it more or less resembles a small minnow.

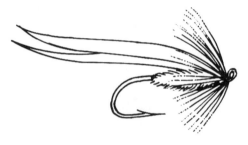

Salt-water lures are more or less like freshwater lures, except that they tend to be, on the average, bigger (for bigger fish) and simpler. This is due to several factors, including:

1. Sea fish don't have normal access to much in the way of small surface-disturbing creatures–insects, frogs, and the like–so splashing, popping, or other surface-disturbing lures are not so much in evidence.

2. Some sea fish, especially those fished for with artificial lures, normally move at such great speeds that they have little time to inspect their prey very closely, and so there is little need to imitate nature too closely, either. The curious device known as the **Swedish Pimple**, a diamond-shaped hunk of shiny metal, doesn't look like anything but a diamond-shaped hunk of metal, but fish bite on it just the same:

Plugs and **spoons** are more or less like freshwater plugs and spoons, only bigger.

Eelskins are rigged with a length of the same kind of chain, consisting of a series of tiny metal balls, that is used for electrical pull chain and retainers for bathtub stoppers, and two or three hooks:

The flexible chain allows the eelskins, when trolled, to wiggle in a quite convincing imitation of a live eel. They are especially favored for striped bass.

There is also a device, essentially a bunch of nylon fluff trailing a piece of metal more or less in the shape of a fish's head:

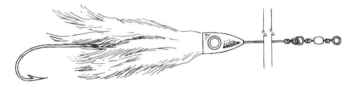

The device is, for some reason, called a **squid**, although in action it resembles a small, improbably-colored fish. (Most of them come in gay colors or color combinations.) The eyes are probably there to impress the purchaser rather than the fish.

* * * * *

Here are a few aspects of artificial lures useful to know about:

1. Non-anglers are sometimes amazed at the enormous number of lures that many fishermen feel obliged to cart around with them when fishing. A certain amount of this can be ascribed to impulse buying–many of the lures that adorn the tackle-boxes of otherwise sane fishermen (especially bass fanatics) have never caught, and will never catch, a single fish, but were bought simply because they look pretty.

However, there is more to it than that. Lures can differ from each other in at least four important respects: type of action (does it flutter, does it wobble gently, or what?), color, size, and depth. Supposing a fisherman, wanting to assemble a collection of lures that will cover most exigencies, starts out with plugs. Assuming further that he restricts himself to no more than three kinds of action, two categories of color–light and dark–two categories of size–large and small–and three categories of depth–deep, medium, and shallow–there he is with thirty-six plugs, and he hasn't even begun with spoons or spinners! Obviously, most anglers don't go quite that far, but you can see how, once you get started, it is hard to stop.

A few comments on the Four Characteristics:

a. **Type of Action**. Every artificial lure that derives its action from being pulled through the water should be tested at various speeds to be sure that you are aware of the speeds at which it works best, and the speeds at which it will not work at all. Wobbling spoons tend to be especially touchy in this respect. I remember having a small fat spoon, consisting of a sliver of abalone shell fixed to a silvery metal backing, pointed out to me as being especially effective for catching cutthroat trout. The claim seemed unduly specific: why just cutthroat? Why not any kind of trout–rainbow, for example? I found it hard to believe that fish with almost identical oxygen needs, feeding habits, and the like would react differently to a particular lure. The mystery was solved when I tried the lure out by trailing it behind a boat. The spoon was so constructed that unless the boat was moving at a pretty good clip, it wouldn't wobble at all. Cutthroat operate at a slightly faster pace than rainbow, and so the spoon operated by default–it was too fast for rainbow, but apparently just the right speed for cutthroat.

b. **Color**. There are two schools of thought about color: School One holds that you should use dark colors on bright days and light colors under conditions of reduced visibility (dark days, twilight, or early dawn); School Two claims the exact opposite–you should use light colors on bright days and dark colors under conditions of reduced visibility. I incline toward School Two. Although tests have established that bass, for example, can distinguish colors to some degree, color does not seem to be anywhere near as important to fish as dark-versus-light under even optimum conditions, and this would certainly be true under conditions of reduced visibility, when color distinctions fade out even for human beings. It is therefore possible that dark colors work best under conditions of reduced visibility because light colors produce a gray-on-gray effect (a little moonlight goes a long way), whereas dark colors produce a more contrasty black-on-gray effect.

c. **Size**. In general, the bigger the fish, the bigger the lure, but this is by no means a law of nature. There are times when a big fish will take only small lures, and sometimes a small fish will strike at a lure almost as big as himself.

d. **Depth**. The depth at which a particular lure moves through the water will depend on one or more of a number of factors: (1) the construction of the lure itself, which may be so made that it dives when pulled through the water, (2) the action of a planing or diving device at the end of the line, to which the lure is attached, (3) the use of lead weights or leaded line, and (4) the speed at which the lure moves through the water. With some diving lures, the faster you move them, the deeper they dive; with others, they just wobble faster. The only way to tell which is which is to try them out.

2. Although plugs, spoons, and flies are true lures in the sense that they are the thing that the fish strikes at, spinners are a little special. They are normally fished either with bait–cut bait or a gob or worms–or with an artificial attractant, usually a bunch of feathers or nylon fiber–what amounts to a simple artificial fly. Apparently what happens is that the fish sees the spinner sparkling away at a distance, and comes closer to investigate; when he does, he sees the bait or artificial lure and, forgetting all else, strikes at it. This phenomenon seems to work with even simpler equipment. I remember one occasion on which another fellow and I were trolling for Spanish mackerel in the Gulf of Mexico. Although we were both using identical lures (red-and-white squid) I was catching twice as many mackerel as he. There was no special technique involved–the only difference was that I had previously been using a spinner, and to prevent the spinner

from twisting the line, I had hung a keel–a simple triangular piece of aluminum weighted on the bottom–onto the line a foot or so ahead of the lure. I had not bothered to remove the keel before changing from a spinner to a squid. Apparently mackerel could see the keel, shining in the bright sunlight, at considerable distances, and upon coming closer to investigate, saw, and struck at, my lure, whereas my partner's lure had to come within the fish's area of vision before it could attract strikes.

3. Many people consider fly fishermen the aristocrats of the confraternity, and fly fishermen of course do nothing to discourage this attitude. However, as far as I can see, the appeal of fly fishing is based, not on such fancy considerations as that it is more sporting to catch a fish with a tiny artificial tied to an extremely fine tippet than with a big, vulgar plug or spoon on a ten-pound line, but rather on the fact that the fly fisherman can see much more clearly what is going on, and hence more directly affect the outcome. The only control a fisherman trolling for striped bass with an eelskin can exert on the outcome is to select the channels where he imagines the striped bass hang out, control the speed at which the lure moves, and attempt to fish the lure at an appropriate depth. If there are any striped bass around, he will never know it unless and until one strikes his lure.

The fly fisherman, especially one working a stream, has a lot more options. He can "read the stream"–study the bends, banks, rocks, and riffles with an eye toward deducing where fish are likely to be. If he sees a lot of mayflies, he can tie on an artificial of the same color, thus "matching the hatch." If he sees a lot of "dimples" occurring on the surface of a pool, he knows that trout are feeding there, so he can drop his fly just above the place where the fish are, being careful not to let the shadow of his line fall on the spot. And so on.

4. Since artificials normally don't have taste or odor, they must depend for their effect purely on visual stimuli. One of the ways animals differ from people is that the animals seem incapable of recognizing a living being unless it can be heard, scented, or *seen to move*. Once while I was sitting on a ridge in a Vermont forest (bucks-only hunting season), a mature white-tailed doe came up to within 10 feet of me. I was in plain sight, and wearing a

red hat, but since I made no sound, I didn't move, and the wind was in the wrong direction, she simply could not interpret the mass of colors and shapes in front of her as something alive. I might as well have been a stump, or a piece of machinery abandoned in the woods.

If this is true of deer, how much more will it be true for fish, with a much simpler brain and nervous system? It therefore seems reasonable to suppose that the single most important requirement for an artificial lure is that it be capable of *behaving in a convincing way*, color and shape being much less important.

With the coming into common use of rubber-mold casting, it became possible to mass-produce extremely convincing facsimiles of all kinds of fish, frogs, crayfish, insects, and other small forms of life presumably of interest to game fish, complete to the minutest detail, but the fish who is to be conned into biting on these creations is not likely to pay much attention to them unless their action bears out the promise of their shape, size, and color pattern.

Anybody who doubts that exact shape doesn't matter has only to inspect a few trout flies. They don't look at all like living insects; the secret of their success (or what success they have) is based, not on their exact shape but on their capacity for putting on a lifelike performance. For a dry fly, putting on a lifelike performance consists largely of floating past where the fish lies and making a convincing imprint on the water. The natural mayfly rides on the water with the end of its abdomen submerged (this is the normal position of the egg-laying female), but the fly is so lightweight that its feet do not break through the water's surface tension. The fish, observing the fly from below, cannot possibly see it as the human eye sees it; he apparently sees it as a vague mass of color or color-pattern–dark or light–upon which is superimposed a cluster of small dimples (produced by the feet) and a medium-sized blob (produced by the end of the abdomen). The hackle, or collar of bristles, on the artificial fly produces the same kind of dimples as those produced by the mayfly's feet, and the downturned hook produces the same kind of blob created by its abdomen.

When an artificial fly has been in the water too long, it gets waterlogged; when this happens, the hackle breaks through the surface tension of the water, the characteristic dimple-and-blob pattern becomes a single, larger blob, and the fish, no longer capable of interpreting what he sees as something edible (or merely something interesting) will ignore it. However, all the fisherman needs do to restore its credibility is to dry it out so it once more rides the water properly.

* * * * *

With all the different kinds of artificial lures there are, the question might well be asked: "How did they happen to be invented? How does one go about devising an artificial lure, anyway?"

The story goes that, in 1830, a fellow named Julio Buel, of Castleton, Vermont, was having lunch while on a fishing trip, and dropped a teaspoon overboard. As the spoon sank, twinkling and wobbling, into the watery depths, he was surprised to see a fish strike at it.

Reasoning that there was something about the movement of the spoon-bowl in the water that was attractive to fish, he got another spoon, sawed off the handle, attached a hook to one end, and his line to the other. Thus was born the Buel Wobbling Spoon, the foundation-stone of a sizeable artificial-lure industry.

A lot of other artificial lures undoubtedly came about in the same sort of casual and semi-accidental way. If so, what is to prevent anybody from inventing his own? Actually, nothing. If you can manage to cobble together a device that induces fish to bite, even if you don't know why it works, that's all that's required. (Julio Buel didn't really know why the fish struck at his teaspoon, either.)

From this circumstance it is but a step to a more glowing vision: an ingenious angler stumbles onto a simple device that has all the finny monsters in the vicinity shouldering each other aside to get at it; the wily angler patents the device, and retires to a life of gilded ease on the proceeds. Perhaps I am being unduly pessimistic, but I seem to recall a saying to the effect that although lawyers and promoters may thrive, inventors usually die broke.

Be that as it may, a while back, on one of the Tuesday evenings my wife devotes to absorbing the soothing sound of hard rubber smiting maple at the bowling alley, I was washing dishes. Among the vessels, utensils, and other artifacts in the dishpan was a cheese-paring knife. It was shaped something like a round-nosed pancake-turner, except that the flat part was bent slightly at a point fairly close to the handle end, and right along the bend was a narrow slot, sharpened on the lower edge. By drawing this device along the top of a slab of any fairly firm cheese, you can shave off extremely thin slices. Well, although no fish surged from the bottom of the dishpan to strike at the cheese-paring knife, its action in the water was, to say the least, interesting, so in due time I got around to making a lure based on the same basic principle.

The process of manufacture goes like this:

1. With a pair of tin snips, cut out a pattern more or less as shown here. The exact size, dimensions, or gauge of metal are apparently not critical.

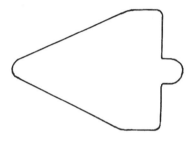

2. Drill holes in the front tip and the trailing tab.

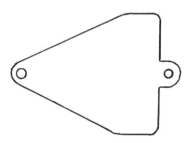

3. Since a slot would probably weaken the lure unduly, drill a row of holes instead:

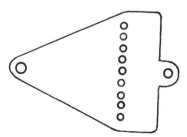

4. Bend slightly along the line of holes, attach a hook by
   means of a split ring, and the lure is complete:

   If you want to paint it–red and white, or frog-pattern
green–bear in mind that most spoons are painted on the
side most often exposed to the fish–in this case, the convex side–leaving the other side shiny.

   This, then, is the Cheese-Paring Lure–actually (despite
its shape) a wobbling spoon. I hope it is unpatentable, but
I am not going to spend the several hundred dollars it
would take to find out. And if in the course of time a
patented facsimile, advertised as the sensational new
Dinky-Popsy, or the famous (as of ten minutes ago)
Mobbler-Wuddler, appears, I will start thinking of common sense as a luxury the average man can no longer
afford.

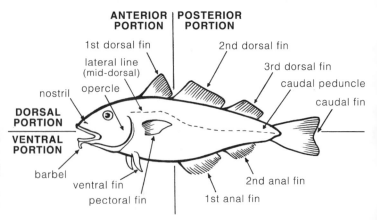

Identifying features of a fish

9. Types of Fish

It is possible to impale some sort of bait on your hook, commit it to the depths of a likely looking body of water, and hope that some sort of fish, type unspecified, will bite on it, but most fishermen worth their salt (and a few salt-free ones I know of) prefer to know in advance what kind of fish they are trying to catch, or, failing that, to identify the fish they have inadvertently caught.

If you consult a source-book on fish, you will probably find that it is taxonomically arranged–that is, arranged according to the categories and sub-categories used to classify all living things: phylum, class, order, family, genus, and species, each of which can be identified by such details as type of scales, type and distribution of teeth, number of spines at various points of its anatomy, and so forth and so on. This is great for a taxonomist, but a little tough on a fisherman, who is likely to be more interested in recognizing a particular kind of fish when he sees it than in laying it out on a slab in the laboratory so he can count the spines on the anal fin and check the presence or absence of vomerine teeth.

Here is one way of doing this:

1. Familiarize yourself with the commonest general types of fish there are. This will not allow you to distinguish, say, the long-eared sunfish from the red-spotted sunfish, McKay's sunfish, the shell-cracker, the red-breasted bream, the pumpkinseed, or even from the stump-knocker, but if you go into too much detail too soon, you will never see the end of it. Start with the general types, and build up familiarity with the particular species as time permits.

2. Familiarize yourself with the kind of water in which the type is normally found. Every species of fish has its limits–the conditions of temperature, pressure, salinity, water movement, degree of oxygenation of the water, available food supply, and the like it must have to survive and maintain a stable population. To a lesser degree of exactitude, the same applies to the general type to which the particular species belongs, so when you look at a particular body of water from the point of view of these criteria, although you may not be able to predict in advance what kinds of fish will inevitably be found in it, you will usually be able to eliminate from consideration the kinds of fish which cannot possibly survive there.

3. Familiarize yourself with the feeding habits of the general types. This will allow you to forecast with some accuracy the kind of bait and fishing techniques to use. A lot of this is just common sense. If you know, for example, that flounder spend most of their time lying on the bottom waiting for food to drift within easy reach, you know in advance that you are not going to catch a flounder by trolling at 20 knots with a surface lure. Similarly, if you are fishing for sunfish in a small pond, there is no point in using a four-inch plug, because even if the size of the plug didn't scare him off, a sunfish couldn't possibly open his mouth wide enough to accommodate a lure that big.

People sometimes make fun of tourists who become instant authorities on the Louvre, the largest art museum in Paris, on the basis of a two-hour visit, pointing out that the only way you could make a tour of all its galleries in that short time, to say nothing of actually looking at the pictures and statues, would be on a motorcycle. Well, in this chapter appears our own motorcycle tour through the piscatorial wing of the Museum of Natural History. A few definitions and clarifications:

1. There is wide variation among the number and type of fins different kinds of fish have, but the following arrangement is most typical: (1) a pair of pectoral fins, corresponding to the forelegs of a mammal, located just behind the gill covers, (b) a pair of ventral fins, corresponding to the hind legs of a mammal, located below the body, (c) one or more dorsal fins along the back, and (d) one or more anal fins on the bottom of the body, just in front of the tail. Of these, the number and type of dorsal fins provides perhaps the best starting point for identification, and for this reason, the system of classification used in this book is based primarily on the number and type of dorsal fins, exceptions being limited to those few cases where some other obvious characteristic is more convenient. It must be borne in mind that this list is incomplete, arbitrary, and unscientific, its only purpose being to help identify fish.

2. It is useful to know in advance about how big the fish is that you are trying to describe. In this list, "small" means "hardly worth frying," "medium-sized" means "up to about five pounds," "large" means "up to 20 or 30 pounds," and "very large" means "so big it's ridiculous."

Of course, all fish are small when newly hatched; the sizes given indicate the probable size when caught.

3. Water categories by temperature are warm, temperate, and cool. In many cases, the temperature preferences of a particular kind of fish can be stated in only the most general way. Although gar are usually considered warm-water fish, they are sometimes found in Canada; although sturgeon are alleged to prefer cool water to spawn in, Atlantic sturgeon thrive in the Pascagoula River, in Mississippi; although tuna are supposed to favor warmer water, they sometimes turn up off Newfoundland. Fish, like people, are not completely predictable.

4. Most fish are either fresh-water, salt-water, or anadromous–that is, they live most of their lives in the ocean, but ascend freshwater streams to spawn. Once in a while, fish that do this get blocked off from access to the sea and become "land-locked"; when this happens, they adjust to a different life cycle, their physical appearance changes somewhat, and they usually don't get as big as they do in the ocean. One kind of eel reverses the process–eels of this species live most of their lives in freshwater lakes and streams along the East Coast but spawn well to the south of Bermuda. In this list, fish are categorized according to the type of water–fresh or salt–in which they are most likely to be caught, rather than according to the type of water in which they spend most time.

5. The terms "bottom-feeder" and "pelagic" are often used to describe fish, especially ocean fish. A bottom-feeder is a fish that stays fairly close to the reefs and banks that provide it with food and cover, while a pelagic fish is one that ranges freely in the open ocean. This is a little like the difference between Virginia white-tail deer, which prefer fairly dense forest cover, and pronghorn antelope, which are found in the open plains.

6. Sharks, rays, and sturgeon are only distantly related to most of the creatures we think of as fish–the ones with bony skeletons–and many Americans are unwilling to believe that freshwater eels are really fish, but since they all bite on bait about as readily as the more conventional kind (when I caught an eel off the breakwater at the junction of the Anacostia and Potomac Rivers, in Washington, D.C., it was hard to tell which of us–the eel or I–was more astonished) they have been included.

FRESH-WATER FISH

SINGLE DORSAL

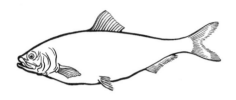

Suckers, Redhorse, Buffalo. Many kinds. Small to medium-sized; warm to cool water. Conformation varies, but most have mouths more or less sucker-like, ranging from "goldfish" to "vacuum-cleaner." Tend to feed on very small plant and animal life; however, can sometimes be caught on worms or doughballs, using small hooks.

Minnows, Chub, Carp. All small except carp; also warm to cool water. So many varieties that it is difficult to generalize physical appearance, but the single dorsal fin is invariable. Because of their small size, sometimes make nuisances of themselves by "stealing bait"–making off with chunks of bait impaled on hooks too big for them to get caught on.

Alewives. Very similar in appearance to the herring (see "Salt-Water"), but anadromous; medium sized; temperate to cool water. Because of their anadromous habit, they are more accessible to the angler than herring; most, however, are netted commercially as they ascend rivers to spawn. A land-locked version is found in the Great Lakes. Usually fished for with bait.

Shad. Not too different in appearance or habitat from alewives, also anadromous, and also netted commercially as they ascend rivers, but they are considerably larger than alewives, and are more highly prized for their table qualities–not only for their flesh, but also for their roe. Originally confined to the Atlantic, they have been successfully transplanted on the West Coast. There is considerable interest in fishing for shad along the Connecticut, Hudson, and Delaware Rivers, using small weighted flies. It occasionally happens that shad are accidentally caught by anglers fishing for salmon, whose spawning waters they sometimes share.

DORSAL, FAR BACK

Gar. Medium to large; warm-water. Several varieties, but gars are unmistakable: extremely long body, with single dorsal fin quite close to the tail; jaws like those of a crocodile, only narrower. They can tolerate brackish water. Bite readily on live or cut bait, but hard to catch, possibly because of hard mouth parts, so they are sometimes fished for with nooses of piano-wire–the bait is hung in the middle of the loop, and when a gar puts his snout through the loop to seize the bait, the wire is pulled tight.

Pike, Pickerel, Muskellunge. Medium to large; most temperate to cool water. Unmistakable: body long and slender, like that of the gar, but instead of the narrow crocodile-mouth of the gar, have broad, deeply-cut jaws armed with formidable teeth. Most kinds come in strongly-marked patterns. Usually fished for with spoons, spinners, plugs, and the like, or live bait.

Sturgeon. Large to very large; anadromous, usually returning to cool freshwater streams. There are several kinds, but the type is unmistakable: covered with large bony plates instead of scales; shovelnosed; upper lobe of the tail much longer than the lower. Definitely bottom feeders, as indicated by the fleshy feelers just ahead of the mouth, but will take spoons and other artificials. San Francisco Bay provides sport fishing for sturgeon

TWO DORSALS, SECOND ADIPOSE (BARBELS)

Catfish, Bullheads, Stone Cats. Small to large–catfish largest, bullheads smaller, stone cats smallest. Mostly warm-water, although the smaller varieties are found in temperate water. (There are warm-water sea catfish too, but they are less common.) Unmistakable: no scales, prominent and numerous barbels (whiskers), two dorsal fins, the second one adipose–like a little fat finger. It is odd that adipose fins are a characteristic mark of two totally unlike groups; on one hand, the frankly ugly catfish and his relatives; on the other, the undeniably handsome salmon, trout, and whitefish. Bottom feeders; normally fished for with bait or odoriferous mixtures (cheese, chicken blood, etc.) that cater to their scavenging habits. In *Walden*, Thoreau mentions that he would sometimes catch "horned pout" (bullheads) "with a bunch of worms strung on a thread." He is referring to a method of catching bullheads without a hook: with a large needle, string many worms lengthwise onto a string; make a ball of the strung worms, lower to the bottom, and leave there for a while; pull up quickly and steadily. The bullheads, being provided with inward-slanting teeth, will be unable to let go quickly enough to get away. (Caution: The dorsal and pectoral fins incorporate spikes that not only can stab you, but are also connected with glands that secrete a substance extremely irritating to human tissue.)

TWO DORSALS, SECOND ADIPOSE (NO BARBELS)

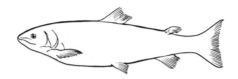

Salmon. Medium to large; cool-water. Several varieties. Salmon, trout, lake trout, whitefish, grayling, and smelt are easily recognized by their dorsal fin arrangement: the first rather far back along the spine, and the second adipose. (Catfish and their relatives, the only other group with this particular arrangement, are easily distinguished by their whiskery barbels and complete lack of scales.) The fish of this group usually have tails more or less "square"–not deeply lobed. The adipose fins are usually small, and are sometimes hard to recognize. Salmon are anadromous, but the angler is likely to encounter them in the freshwater streams they ascend in order to spawn. It is a curious fact that they do not feed while in the spawning phase, and hence it must be something other than hunger that impels them to strike at salmon flies–irritation, perhaps. For the same reason, the technique of "matching the hatch," common in trout fishing, is not much favored; the thing to do is to keep trying different specimens until something connects.

Trout, Lake Trout. Small to medium; cool-water. Mostly freshwater, although a few are anadromous. (The steelhead is a rainbow trout that has taken up the anadromous life.) Trout tend to inhabit streams or smaller freshwater lakes; lake trout seem to prefer larger, deeper lakes. (The kamloops is a rainbow trout that has changed over to a lake-trout way of life, become stouter, and lost the pinkish-purplish streak along the side that gives the rainbow its name.) Although many traditionalists will fish for trout with nothing but flies, the trout itself is less fussy; it will also bite on other artificials or worms. Except for short periods in spring and late fall, lake trout (and landlocked salmon as well) are usually so deep that they must be trolled for with weighted lines.

Grayling. Small to medium. Like trout in most respects, but first dorsal fin plume-shaped and greatly enlarged.

Whitefish, Cisco. Whitefish, medium to large; cisco, small to medium. Conformation somewhat like that of salmon, but with larger scales and proportionately smaller mouths; habits like those of lake trout.

Smelt. Small. In appearance a cross between a trout and an anchovy (see under "Salt-Water"), having the typical trout dorsal fin arrangement and the anchovy's slender body. It is anadromous, and is normally caught in the course of "smelt runs"–when smelt ascend streams to spawn, they often do so in such numbers that they can be scooped up with dip nets. However, they can also be caught by means of more conventional tackle, using small baits such as shrimp. (A landlocked version is widely fished for through the ice on Lake Champlain.)

Burbot. Medium-sized, cool-water. A freshwater version of the hake (see "Salt-Water"). Appearance and habits similar. Usually fished for with bait.

SPINY-RAY DORSAL

Largemouth Bass, Smallmouth Bass, Spotted Bass. Not to be confused with sea bass. Medium-sized; warm to temperate water. Body oblong, mouth very large (the mouth of the small-mouthed bass is large; the mouth of the large-mouthed bass is larger). The spiny-ray dorsal is characteristic: it looks like two fins that have started to grow together–the front one spiky, and the back one softer. Largemouths and smallmouths have somewhat different habits: largemouths seem to have greater tolerance for still, shallow, warm (and hence not necessarily clear) water, and will feed either deep or in the shallows; smallmouths seem to be more insistent on moving, deeper, cooler water, and hence are less often fished for with surface lures. The spotted bass looks pretty much like a largemouth and is alleged to behave more like a smallmouth.

Crappie. Small to medium, same kind of waters as largemouth. Similar dorsal fin arrangement, but body shorter, more humpbacked; mouth proportionately smaller. Behaves much like a miniature bass; will take small artificials.

Sunfish, Rock Bass, Bluegill, Pumpkin-seed. Small to medium. Very many varieties, some brightly colored. Again, like bass except in size and shape: same spiny-ray dorsal, but body even shorter than that of crappie–almost as high as long. Since their mouths are proportionately even smaller than those of crappie, usually fished for with bait, although they will take small flies.

White Bass, Yellow Bass. Like slightly elongated sunfish; similar dorsal fin arrangement, with narrow darkish lengthwise stripes, more conspicuous, if anything, than the stripes of the striped bass (see under "Salt-Water"). Usually found in deeper water than sunfish.

MODIFIED SPINY-RAY DORSAL

Yellow Perch. Small to medium; temperate water. Shaped vaguely like a humpbacked, slightly elongated bass with a ski-slide nose. The spiny-ray backfin is similar, except that, instead of being run together, as in the case of the bass and his relatives, it is definitely two separate fins. Markings unmistakable: dark bars against yellowish background. Will bite readily on all kinds of bait, a worm trailed behind a small spinner being especially effective. In winter, can be fished for through the ice, a much-favored bait being, for some reason, the eyeball of another yellow perch.

Wall-Eyed Pike, Sauger. Physically very much like an elongated yellow perch, same backfin arrangement, but with less definite markings–hence its occasional name: pike-perch. The sauger is pretty much like the wall-eye, only smaller. Like the yellow perch, walleyes can be fished for through the ice, usually with live minnows as bait.

DORSAL TAIL CONTINUITY

Eel. Small to medium-sized. In a curious reversal of the anadromous habit, spend most of their lives in temperate to cool streams and lakes, but go to sea to spawn. (There are saltwater eels too–congers and morays–of relatively little interest to fishermen.) Unmistakable: if it is found in fresh water, and has a mouth like a fish and a body like a snake, it's an eel. Although highly regarded in Europe and Asia, they are not much eaten in the United States. Their "snake-like" appearance may have something to do with it. Usually caught with bait.

SALT-WATER FISH

SINGLE DORSAL

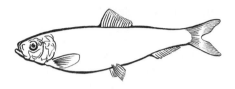

Pilchard. In appearance much like herring (which see). Those caught commercially and canned as "sardines" are small, but mature individuals attain perhaps 10 inches. Temperate to cool water. Since they feed mostly on plankton, they are of little interest to anglers.

Anchovy. If you come across a small, silvery fish whose deeply-cut jaw and disproportionately large eye give it an air of gloom and pessimism, it is probably an anchovy. Warm to cool water. Like pilchards, they travel in large schools, and are extensively netted by commercial fishermen.

Herring. Difficult to describe because it is so nondescript: spindle-shaped body, fairly large scales, deeply-forked tail. If you told a child, "draw a fish," he would probably produce a fairly accurate picture of a herring. Small to medium; temperate to cool waters. Also travel in schools, also extensively netted. The young, like pilchards, are canned as "sardines"; mature herring usually wind up salted, dried, or pickled.

Menhaden. Like herring with a few dark spots, except that their heads present a distinctively "bone-headed" appearance. They are extensively netted commercially, but are made into fertilizer and fish oil rather than being used for food for man. Small to medium; warm to cool water.

Bonefish. Like menhaden, has a very bony head, but a slimmer body and a pointed nose. Medium to large, preferring warm, shallow water. Although much favored by anglers because of their fighting qualities, they are considered inedible.

Tarpon. Unmistakable: extremely large scales, a blunt, "bulldog" mouth, and a dorsal fin terminating in an extremely long whip-like extension. (The thread herring, a relative of the common herring–there are Atlantic and Pacific varieties–is perhaps the only other fish with this type of dorsal fin.) Large to very large. Like bonefish, prefers warm water, is favored by anglers because of its fighting qualities, and is considered inedible.

Flying Fish. Unmistakable: the lower lobe of the tail is longer than the upper, and the pectoral fins have been modified into broad, translucent wings; by briskly wiggling their tails as they emerge from the surface, flying fish can propel themselves into the air for considerable distances, in order to escape from large, fast game fish, which seem to be particularly fond of them. Medium-sized; favor warm to temperate water. Thor Heyerdahl, in *Kon-Tiki*, reports that flying fish sometimes landed on the deck of his raft when he was making his Pacific voyage, providing a welcome addition to the menu.

SINGLE DORSAL, LONG

Dolphin. The terminology is a little confusing–there is also a seagoing mammal, actually one of the smaller whales, called the dolphin–but the fish itself is unmistakable: greenish-gold in color (hence the Spanish name, "dorado") with a single extremely long fin along its back. The nose of the male is blunt and squared off something like that of a sperm whale; that of the female is more conventionally fish-like. Medium to large; primarily warm-water.

Blenny. Many kinds. If you find a small fish with a single fin all along its back and a round tail, in shallow salt water, chances are it is a blenny. Warm to cold water.

Wolffish. Has the same kind of dorsal fin and tail as the blenny, but medium to large. Primarily a cold-water fish. Warning: Since it feeds primarily on shellfish, the strong jaws and formidable teeth it uses to crush oyster shells can amputate a finger with the greatest of ease. Despite its odd appearance, it is edible, but since "wolffish" doesn't sound very appetising, it is sold commercially under other names, much as, in the fur business, rabbit is known as "lapin" and sheepskin masquerades as "mouton."

SPINY-RAY DORSAL

Grunts, Pigfish. Small to medium; warm-water; many brightly striped. They look a little like sea bass or freshwater white bass with bigger heads and deeper jaws. Like most others in this group, bottom feeders.

Snapper, Schoolmaster. Resemble grunts (to which they are related) but tend to run slightly larger. Mostly warm-water. Bottom feeders, favoring crabs and shrimp. They are highly regarded for their table qualities.

Porgy, Scup. Similar in appearance to grunts and snappers–possibly slightly chunkier, with smaller, but much stronger jaws, to enable them to feed on molluscs and crustaceans. Warm to temperate water.

Sea-Perch. Because of their nondescript appearance, hard to describe with precision; about all that can be said about them is that they are similar in appearance to freshwater sunfish, but with, in general, simpler color patterns. Warm to temperate water; medium to large.

Grouper. If sea-perch are the seagoing version of freshwater sunfish, grouper look something like small-mouth bass, except that their heads are larger in proportion to their bodies. Mostly warm-water; medium to large.

Sea Bass, Jewfish. In general conformation, very like grouper, but larger–up to 500 or 600 pounds. Mostly warm-water. Jewfish are much favored by skin-diving spear fishermen, possibly because they combine great size (and hence impressiveness as a trophy) with ease of approach (when approached, they seem more curious than frightened).

MODIFIED SPINY-RAY DORSAL

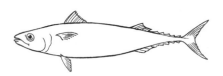

Goby. Just as a small fish with a single ribbon-like dorsal fin and a rounded tail, found in shallow salt water, is usually a blenny, a fish that is also small, also found in shallow salt water, and also has a more or less rounded tail, but sports two separate dorsal fins, is probably a goby. (There are a few gobies that get to be medium-sized, but they are rare.) Mostly warm-water.

Mullet. More or less silvery, blunt-nosed, with big eyes and small mouths. Schooling fish, medium, preferring shallow, warm water, where they feed on plant life. They have the habit of jumping out of the water when disturbed. Because of their vegetarian habits, they do not bite readily on most conventional baits, but can sometimes be caught on dough-balls, using very small hooks.

Croakers, Drum. More or less chunky-bodied, often with conspicuous nostrils. Some of them have chin barbels. As their names suggest, they are capable of making grunting or groaning noises when caught. Mostly small to medium (though drum sometimes are large); warm to temperate waters. Feed on shellfish, crustaceans, and small fish.

Whiting, Corbina. Actually kinds of croakers, but somewhat longer in the body. They are similar in feeding habits, and have a single chin barbel. Corbina are confined to the West Coast.

Weakfish. Still another kind of croaker, even longer in the body, but minus the chin barbel. The only thing weak about the weakfish is his jaw–if the fisherman tugs too hard on the line, the hook will tear loose. Warm to temperate waters; medium size. Also known as "squeteague." There is a variety, with dark spots on the upper half of the body and tending to prefer warmer water, that is sometimes rather confusingly referred to as "sea trout."

Snook. Unmistakable. Slender, mostly silvery fish, with a pronounced dark line along its sides and yellowish fins and tail. The nose is sharply pointed, with an undershot jaw. Medium; warm water. A game fish.

Striped Bass. Like grouper, vaguely similar in shape to freshwater bass, except that the spiny dorsal fin is distinct from the softer one. The longitudinal stripes are fairly well defined, silvery-bluish and dark. Large to very large, temperate waters. A highly prized game fish.

Bluefish. The head half resembles that of a bass, but the tail half resembles that of a jack (which see), with long, soft fins both above and below the body and a deeply-cut, V-shaped tail. Medium; temperate water. A truly voracious creature, which will attack and kill more than it can possibly eat. Often fished for in the surf, where it goes in pursuit of small fish.

Barracuda. Unmistakable. In general appearance, the seagoing version of the pike, pickerel, and muskellunge–elongated body, and big jaws with formidable teeth. Medium to large, mostly warm-water. The larger ones can be dangerous to swimmers or scuba divers. Bite readily on bait or artificials.

TWO DORSALS

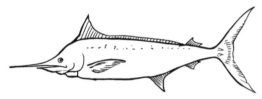

Marlin. Unmistakable. The first dorsal fin is very long, narrow, and pointed in front, while the second is small and far back; the body is torpedo-shaped; and the upper lip is provided with a rapier-like spike, used to stun small fish preparatory to feeding on them. Large to very large; warm to temperate water. Avidly sought by trophy fishermen. (The monster fish in Hemingway's *The Old Man and the Sea* was a marlin.)

Sailfish. Very like marlin, except that the first dorsal is broad and ragged-looking, something like the sail of a Chinese junk.

Swordfish. Has the same high-speed conformation but the "sword" which is the extension if its upper lip is longer and broader in comparison to body length than the marlin's "rapier"; the first dorsal, shaped like a half crescent moon, is directly behind the head, while the second, close to the tail, is hardly there at all. Large to very large; warm to temperate water.

Shark. Many kinds, of various sizes and conformations, with feeding habits ranging from "scavenger" through "man-eater," but the dorsal fin pattern is fairly reliable: the first dorsal is usually shaped much like that of the swordfish, but farther along the back, and the second is small and near the tail. All sharks have, instead of single gill-covers of the bony fishes, multiple vertical gill-slits resembling the ventilating louvers on the hoods of old-fashioned automobiles. Medium to very large; warm to temperate waters. Some people claim that sharks are not particularly aggressive, but in view of their size and the fact that their jaws are invariably lined with several rows of razor-sharp teeth, the prospect of a shark nibbling idly at a swimmer's ankle out of nothing more than curiosity is still not reassuring.

TWO DORSALS, FINLETS

Mackerel, Wahoo. Obviously designed for speed–in addition to having deeply forked tails, joined onto a torpedo-shaped body, all members of this group have a row of more or less well-developed finlets on the dorsal and ventral sides of the body, just in front of the tail. These finlets have an unusual function. It is a commonplace of marine design that the shape of a boat's hull imposes an effective ceiling on the speed at which it can move through the water, no matter how much propulsive force is applied to it: in the same way, the basic shape of the fish's body would impose a similar ceiling on its speed, were it not for the finlets, which allow the water to be left behind more rapidly than would otherwise be the case. (This same principle is sometimes invoked in aircraft design.) Most members of this group are boldly spotted or striped. Medium to large; warm to cool waters. They are considered to be some of the world's best game fish. Most mackerel travel in schools; wahoo are more solitary.

Tuna, Albacore, Bonito, Skipjack. A larger, less brightly patterned version of the mackerel, also traveling in schools, also having the same kind of finlets. Large to very large; warm to temperate waters. Also highly prized as game fish.

STRIP DORSAL AND ANAL

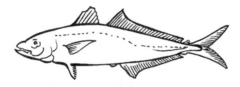

Jack. These and the others in the group are distinguished by a long fin along the dorsal side, and another, of equal or nearly equal length, on the ventral side, beginning at or slightly behind the middle of the body, and extending almost to the tail. Jack also have a small spiny dorsal fin just ahead of the long fin, and, like all other members of the group, have a deeply-forked tail. Small to large; warm to temperate water.

Pompano, Permit. These are jacks too, but with a rounded nose, something like a less extreme version of the male dolphin's. Small to medium; warm-water. Permit are slightly larger. Pompano are highly prized for their table qualities.

Lookdown, Moonfish. More jacks, but of a radically different shape. If you took a sunfish, chopped off its head on a downward-sloping diagonal, located a pair of eyes just inside the middle of the cut-off line, and relocated its mouth at the bottom of the cut, you would have recreated the general shape of a moonfish or lookdown. Small; warm-water. Lookdowns have long, trailing points on the leading edges of their long fins; moonfish lack these adornments.

Butterfish, Harvestfish. Aside from its long fins and tail, butterfish are shaped almost exactly like watermelon seeds. Mouths *very* small. Harvestfish have trailing points on the leading edges of their long fins; butterfish do not. Small; warm to cool waters.

Ling, Hake. Very similar to cod (see below) but the second and third dorsal, and the first and second anal fin have been merged. Some have a single chin barbel; others do not. Medium to large; warm to temperate waters.

3 DORSALS

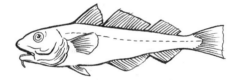

Cod, Pollock, Haddock. Unmistakable–the three dorsal and two anal fins are characteristic. All members of this group are bottom feeders, have a single chin barbel, and are commercially fished. Medium to large, temperate to cool waters.

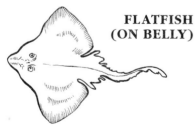

FLATFISH (ON BELLY)

Ray, Skate, Manta. Very many kinds, of various shapes–round, square or butterfly-shaped. Small to very large; warm to cool waters. Most are bottom-feeders, but the manta or devilfish, the largest of them all, is a surface feeder. Some rays have poisonous spines in their tails, with which they can inflict painful wounds.

Sawfish. Unmistakable. A kind of ray, but distinguished by its long, flattened snout, furnished with tooth-like spikes. It feeds by swimming into a school of small fish, slashing at them with its "saw," and then devouring those killed or wounded. Large to very large; warm waters.

FLATFISH (ON SIDE)

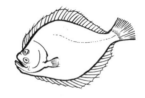

Sole, Plaice, Dab, Turbot, Flounder, Halibut. Many kinds, but unmistakable. Their ancestors were probably free-swimming, but in the course of evolution their swim bladders became less buoyant and hence many of them have passive feeding habits, lying on the bottom and waiting for food to drift by. Others, like halibut, actively pursue their prey. Because of their bottom-dwelling habits, their bottom sides are white or light-colored, while their top sides are darker, and all of them can change color and pattern to match the bottom on which they are lying. Medium to very large; warm to cool waters. Important food fish.

10. Fish Behavior

If you have heard enough stories about old Crook-Jaw, the incredibly shrewd bass that usually hangs about the west end of Lake Swampy, or Old Slit-Tail, the wily brown trout, resident philosopher in Soapkettle Pool on Slickbottom Creek, you might get the idea that fish are pretty intelligent. Maybe so, but it is also possible that the reason why fish have acquired their reputation for sagacity is because it is to the advantage of all fishermen, without exception, not only to believe that fish are pretty smart, but to persuade other people of the same thing–the unsuccessful fisherman, in order to depersonalize his unsuccess, and the successful fisherman, in order to add luster to his prowess.

Rachel Carson, author of *Silent Spring* and *The Sea Around Us*, once pointed out that a small green sea worm, *Convoluta roscoffensis,* which in its native habitat emerges from the sand when the tide goes out and burrows back when the tide comes in, continues to maintain the same routine when transferred to an aquarium, where the influence of the tides cannot possibly be felt. If an attendant at the aquarium, an intelligent being, wanted to know whether the tide was in or out, he would either have to go down to the beach or consult a tide chart, but the worm knows automatically. How does *Convoluta roscoffensis* do it? It can only be that this tiny worm, as Mrs. Carson says, "without a brain, or what we would call a memory, or even any very clear perception," has been provided by Nature with a complex and highly efficient survival mechanism that Man does not yet understand.

Fish, too, have a few surprises up their sleeves–or wherever it is that fish conceal surprises. When it comes time for a salmon to spawn, after spending a year or several years in the ocean, he will not only be able to find the same river he descended as a smolt; he will refuse to spawn in any of its many branches except the particular one, possibly many miles from the sea, in which he spent his extreme youth. We now know that he recognizes his native brook because of its odor, but this doesn't help much. It simply leads to the next question: how can a sense of smell, in a fish or in any other animal, be so finely tuned as to distinguish between the East and West Branches of an obscure brook? As in the case of *Convoluta roscoffensis*, we simply do not know.

The more deeply you go into the matter, the more obvious it becomes that fish are "machines for survival"; if they depended on intelligence to survive, they would all be extinct, but in the process of evolution they have somehow managed to develop all sorts of protective mechanisms, some of them quite complex, by means of which they seem to solve their problems about as well as if they had better sense. For this reason, the more we can find out about the mechanisms that govern the activities that fish indulge in, the better able we will be to catch them consistently.

If all fish reacted the same way to the same stimuli, fishing techniques would be few and simple, but since there are so many kinds, and there is so much variance in response between one species and another, technique can get very complicated indeed. A few of the factors bearing on fish behavior in this connection are listed below. It will be noted that many of the examples contrast bass and trout. This is because bass and trout represent in many ways opposite poles in freshwater-fish behavior, with many other species being found somewhere in between.

1. **Motivation.** It would seem reasonable to suppose that the only reason a fish strikes at a bait or lure is because he imagines it is edible, and wants to eat it. However, this is not always true.

a. When freshwater bass breed, they build nests, which the male guards, and any small creature approaching the nest is driven off. Since the only way a bass can attack is with its mouth, it is probable that defense of its territory, rather than hunger, sometimes induces bass and other nest-building fish to strike at a fisherman's lure.

b. Although it has been definitely established that salmon do not feed while in the breeding phase, they will strike at, and be caught on, artificial flies. It could be boredom, or simple curiosity, or absent-mindedness, but I think it's irritation. Spawning is a serious business: I think that when a salmon strikes at a fly, he doesn't want to eat it–he wants to annihilate it.

c. Many years ago, I arrived, late in the afternoon, at a lake I had never visited before. Being reluctant to postpone the pleasure of seeing what the lake had to offer until the following day, and since I wasn't about to start the ritual of launching the boat with so little daylight left,

I tossed a small lure–a gold spoon, a pear-shaped wooden bead, painted orange, and a treble hook–into a weedy patch off to one side of the dock. A fish hit the lure hard as soon as it touched the water. When I hauled it out, it proved to be a rainbow trout, but I was astonished to find it was only four or five inches long. I released it, and tried again. Bam! Same business. This kept on until I had caught and released five or six midget trout. Their manner of hitting the lure was quite different from the more deliberate way a rainbow inhales a worm or salmon-egg, or even a dry fly, and the interval between the lure hitting the water and the strike allowed no time for the fish to inspect the lure for edibility. It is therefore probable that something about the appearance of the lure in the water immediately triggered an attack response in the fish that had nothing to do with hunger.

2. **Sensitivity to "Natural Presentation."** It has been observed that, in general, baits that are presented to fish in such a way as to imitate nature as closely as possible have a better chance of success than those presented to fish in less sophisticated ways. The sensitivity of any particular fish to naturalness of presentation seems to vary in response to two primary criteria: species and age.

a. **Species.** If, while fishing with a conventional hook-line-sinker-and-float combination, you impale a worm on the hook and arrange your tackle so the worm is suspended about a foot off the bottom, minnows will attack the worm with enthusiasm and abandon, sunfish will be more circumspect, and trout will probably stay away by the thousands. Why some species should be fussier than others in this respect would be hard to say, but there is probably something in the collective memory of some species (stronger in some species than others) that warns the individuals of that species away from unnatural presentations. To call this *suspicion* is perhaps going too far in the direction of assuming that fish think like people–rather than coming to any conclusions about the lethal intent of the clearly-visible hardware, perhaps the trout simply has trouble interpreting the worm as something edible, unless it is on the bottom, where it naturally belongs.

In general, sea fish tend to be much less sensitive toward naturalness of presentation than freshwater fish, probably because several millennia of exposure to the wholesale carnage that goes on in the ocean, leaving so many bits and pieces of edible protein sloshing about at all depths, has made them reckless.

b. **Age.** For any fish normally sensitive to naturalness of presentation, the older he gets, the more necessary it is for the fisherman to present the bait naturally. This may be true for more than one reason:

(1) If you put a pike into a tank together with a few dozen baby trout, it will probably not be long before the pike has eaten them all. Even though there is plenty of material in the tank under which to take shelter, it seems that really small trout do not normally interpret the presence of a big fish in the tank as threatening, and make little or no effort to hide.

However, it is possible to teach baby trout to beware of big fish. If you put a few dozen baby trout into a tank in which there is a big piece of tin roughly cut into the form of a fish, and wired so as to be surrounded by a magnetic field, they will one by one heedlessly swim into the magnetic field and receive a mild shock. Every time this happens, the trout in question will dart away and hide under something, and sooner or later all of them will have been conditioned to avoid large, fish-shaped objects.

If you *then* introduce a pike into the tank, few, if any, of the trout will be eaten, because the presence of the pike acts on them pretty much as the presence of the electrified tin fish does. It is therefore evident that fish, simple creatures though they may be, do learn, and it is highly probable that, within the limits of its normal life span, the bigger a fish gets, the warier he becomes.

(2) The bigger a fish gets, the less frequently he feeds, and the more protein he needs per feeding to make it worth his while. No eight-pound bass is going to heave his mightly bulk out of a well-chosen hiding place if the message put out by a poorly-presented lure is "might be a little food here"; he will respond only if the message is "big, tempting morsel here."

3. **Concealment.** There are fish that do not seem to alarm easily, like the giant manta ray, which is just too big to have many enemies, and a few creatures that are too prickly or poisonous to be edible, but most fish will avoid what looks to them like danger if they can. Since there is

nothing to hide behind in the open sea, small pelagic fish can survive only by outswimming their enemies (or actually jumping right out of the water, like mullet or flying fish), taking refuge in water too shallow for larger predatory fish to follow, or simply by reproducing rapidly enough so that the rate of reproduction can keep up with the rate of attrition. Some bottom-feeders, like some of the side-to-bottom flatfish, are capable of changing their color to match the bottom on which they are lying, but a great many species, especially the freshwater ones, are more or less dependent on concealment for their protection.

Concealment may be provided by weed-beds or rocks in the water, extreme depth, or the darkness of night. The presence or absence of these types of concealment has a considerable effect on the reactions of any particular species of normally concealment-prone fish. An example of this is found in the contrast between fishing for rainbow trout in different kinds of water.

In the State of Washington, there are some fairly deep lakes fed by underground streams, in which rainbow can get all the oxygen they need at just about any depth.

You can still-fish for them: anchor your boat over a sandy bottom thirty or forty feet down; toss in a few salmon eggs as come-on; let down a single salmon egg with a tiny, gold-plated hook concealed inside it; then wait awhile. If you see oily spots appear on the surface, this is a sign that the fish have found your come-on eggs; every time a trout chomps down on an egg, a drop of oil escapes and rises to the surface, and the chances are it won't be long before you have a bite. The presence of shiny objects near the bait, like a metal snap fastening the leader to the line, doesn't seem to matter–that far down, the light is dim, and the fish apparently feel secure.

Or, especially on sunny days, you can surface-troll for them, using an assemblage of several spinners in a row, trailed by just about anything–a minnow, a worm, or a small fly. The purpose of all this shiny hardware is to attract the attention of fish at some distance–they're normally at considerable depths, and one small spinner wouldn't stand much chance of being noticed. The trouble with this method is that the monstrous contraption used sets up such terrific drag that if, as sometimes happens, a really small trout tackles your lure, you could haul him around all afternoon, unaware that you had got a bite.

None of this information helps you much on a really

shallow river. The White River in Arkansas–or anyway the stretch of it that I happened to fish–is swift but shallow, so the best way to fish it is with a john-boat, like a long, narrow rowboat with both ends square, built to ride high in the water. It was on the White that I learned the hard way why the same kind of rainbow trout that, in Washington, will recklessly tackle a complex of whirling blades twice as long as he is will suddenly become, in Arkansas, timid and retiring. On the White, if artificials work, they work; if not, and you want to tie on a worm instead, the only way to do it is to let your boat drift, insure that your hook is japanned black and that your leader is tied to the line rather than secured with a metal snap, loop on the worm, pinch on *one* split-shot weight (which, being black, won't show up much), toss the worm into the water, and let it tumble in the current. The water is only a foot or two deep, every pebble and weed is clearly visible through the gin-clear water, and the current is so swift that weeds are few. In the absence of reasonable cover, a trout is apparently no more anxious to investigate a slightly unnatural-looking bait than a burglar would be to work on a safe in a spotlighted show-window.

4. **Temperature.** There are at least two aspects of temperature of which anglers should be aware: effect on feeding habits and effect on location of feeding grounds.

a. **Effect on Feeding Habits.** The ice fishermen of Lake Champlain catch smelt and yellow perch all winter long, which seems to indicate that smelt and yellow perch will continue to bite no matter how cold it gets. In Louisiana, bass and sunfish will bite when the temperature of the bayous is like that of warm soup, and the air temperature is so high that unless you put your catch on ice at once, it will spoil before you can get it home, which seems to indicate that bass and sunfish will sometimes bite no matter how warm it gets. But trout and their relatives are provided with more sensitive thermostats: if the temperature of the water is either too cold or too warm, they will quite feeding. Not only are all trout fussy that way; some are even fussier than others, the precisely determinable limits of their temperature tolerance being characteristic for each species.

There was the time on Priest Lake, in northern Idaho,

when a buddy and I were fishing for kamloops. The best time to fish for kamloops, an oversized, silvery form of the rainbow trout, is allegedly after the winter ice has broken up but before the spring run-off has made the water so muddy that the kamloops can no longer clearly see the silvers, the small, sharp-nosed fish on which it normally breakfasts, lunches, and dines. When we arrived, the temperature of the water was 34°F, a few degrees shy of the point at which the kamloops' digestive juices normally start flowing, so the locals shook their heads mournfully as we headed off over the gloomy waters, enlivened now and then by a flurry of snow. Luckily, the dolly varden, a more gaily-embroidered cousin of the mighty kamloops, manages to scare up an appetite of sorts slightly above freezing point, so we caught four, ranging in weight from an estimated five to ten pounds. (My more optimistic companion estimated seven to twenty pounds.) Hauling in a dolly varden at such temperatures is attended by all the drama incident to hauling in a submerged log–the poor beasts are so stiff they can scarcely move.

   b. **Effect of Location of Feeding Ground.** In Washington State there is a small lake whose nearness to where I was living at the time made up for the fact that it was no big deal as fishing waters go. It was a little too short on oxygen for trout, but there were a few bass and lots of crappie and assorted small sunfish.

   On the west bank was a stream emptying into a small bay overshadowed by trees, with convenient boulders here and there. On the east bank, some unimaginative farmer had cleared away all trees and brush, leaving a bluff bank leading up to an open field. There weren't even any water-weeds to provide concealment.

   In the summer, the best place to fish from was from the bay on the west bank. The trees there kept the water cool; the rocks and boulders provided concealment; and the stream provided a little trickle of food. The portion of the east bank directly opposite was pretty hopeless–the water exposed to the full force of the sun, no concealment whatever, no special source of food.

   But in the winter, there was a change of rules. Most fish living in a four-season habitat, like most people in the same situation, like to stay comparatively warm in the winter and comparatively cool in the summer, so the requirement was no longer to find the coolest, but the warmest, spot in the lake; with a few inches of ice on the surface, the lack of concealment didn't matter, and the stream was no longer an advantage, the flow of edible protein having ceased. Accordingly, some time between late fall and early winter, the fish gradually moved on over to the east bank, and if you fished the west bank in winter you would fish in vain.

5. **Interference by Man.** The ways in which man can make life difficult for fish are legion: the action of outboard-motor propellers can cut back and eventually destroy the weed-beds that formerly provided hunting habitat for pickerel and wall-eyed pike; by manipulating the gates of dams, man can raise and lower the water level so that the eggs laid in the shallows by spawning fish are exposed to the sun, dry out, and fail to hatch; man can cause or allow the seepage of poisonous chemicals into the water. Incidentally, if you own a pond with fish in it, it is a good idea to warn your nearest and dearest in advance that the answer to the question of whether it is all right to dump just a teentsy-weentsy bit of dirty detergent water into the fishpond is Absolutely Not.

Once again, the kind and degree of modification of fish behavior that results from interference by man will vary widely by species, with bass and trout at opposite ends of the hardiness spectrum. On the kind of lake where boats fitted with the noisiest possible motors towing waterskiers crisscross the waters from dawn till dusk, where the shrieks of too many bathers mingle with the over-amplified tones of non-music, and where flotillas of empty beer-cans float by, it sometimes happens that at about two o'clock in the morning, a solitary boat can be seen slipping away from one of the docks. In the boat is a wily angler who knows that the bass, which have spent the day in the deepest channels of the lake to escape the racket and hullabaloo, have emerged, and are now ranging the shallows to feed on minnows.

6. **Availability of Oxygen.** A fish's gills enable him to extract oxygen from the water, somewhat as the lungs of mammals extract oxygen from the air. The efficiency with which a particular fish's breathing apparatus does the job varies widely among different species. At one end of the scale is a kind of catfish, a relatively recent newcomer to Florida, which has been observed in the act of crossing

suburban lawns, hitching himself along by means of his pectoral fins, apparently commuting from one pool to another. (The lung fish can do better than that: he can survive the dry season of his native land by burrowing into the mud of the pond in which he lives, which then dries to the consistency of poor-grade brick, but there are no lung fish in the United States.) At the other extreme are the trout, the salmon, and their relatives, who must have strongly oxygenated water all the year round if they are to survive.

7. **Intangibles.** Anybody who has fished in the company of many other anglers at the same time–along a dock, perhaps, or as a member of an assemblage of ice fishermen–cannot fail to have noticed that sometimes, following a period during which not much of anything happens for hours at a time, there is a brief, sudden flurry of activity for which there seems to be no rational explanation. For no particular reason, a large number of fish seem to take the notion to bite all at the same time. Sunspots? Witchcraft? Hard to say.

There seems to be some evidence that a change in atmospheric pressure might sometimes be involved. A few years ago, I was staying for a week at a small lake in northern Vermont. It was late in the season, and the water was so shallow (and hence warm) that fishing for trout was pretty much a waste of time. However, unlike Thoreau in his later years, when given the choice between fishing a lake and sitting and admiring its tranquil beauty, I will invariably fish it, no matter how dismal the prospects. One day, I was whipping the waters from the vantage point of a rock jutting picturesquely out into the lake. I think I was using some sort of small wobbling spoon. After a while, I noticed what looked like a cold front approaching from the opposite shore. The wind rose, and began slapping small wavelets against the beach, bringing with it a spatter of rain. Immediately, a fish struck. When I had secured him (he was a frying-size brook trout) and tossed out the spoon again, another fish struck. By the time I had secured *him* and tossed out the spoon again, the wind had dropped. That was it for the day. I kept at it for a while, but the party was over.

From the above, we have seen that the forces that make fish behave as they do are many. Angling know-how consists largely of putting all these factors together–of

knowing whether it is likely that there will be fish in a
given body of water; if so, of what kind; if of a given kind
or kinds, where they are most likely to congregate, and
whether they are likely to bite at that particular moment.

Supposing you arrive at a particular lake in the temperate zone in the middle of July.

1. **Are There Fish in It?** The lake is fair-sized–20
acres or so. Unless grossly polluted, any lake that size
ought to have *some* sort of fish in it. Diagnosis: Very
Probable.

2. **What Kind of Fish?** Every kind has its own peculiar requirements, so let us assume that you will settle for
nothing less than trout. Well, although there are few
streams emptying into the lake, and those are small, the
water is clear, the banks are well wooded, the only signs
of human activity are a few scattered cabins and the marks
of boats on the beach of the access area, and the way the
land slopes toward the water seems to indicate that the
water is fairly deep. The clarity of the water and the
apparently low level of human activity speak well for (but
do not prove) the absence of significant pollution, and the
presumed depth of the lake and the presence of foliage
near the shore will tend to keep the temperature from rising excessively. The amount of heavily-oxygenated water
brought in by streams, the presumed depth of the lake
(although, as we shall see below, depth alone is not
enough to insure adequate oxygenation), and the fact that
no above-water weeds are visible (decaying vegetable
matter uses up oxygen, and excessively large quantities of
last year's dead weeds in the water can seriously deplete
the available oxygen supply) allow the diagnosis: Trout
Possible.

3. **Where Are They?** To answer this question, it will
be necessary (a) to realize that a trout's need for cool,
heavily oxygenated water is not merely a preference, but
a matter of life and death; (b) to understand the normal
distribution of cool and highly oxygenated water in the
kind of lake under discussion.

In late fall, the drop in air temperature cools the surface of the lake. Since cool water is heavier than warm
water, the cooler water sinks to the bottom; warmer water,

thus exposed, also cools and sinks in its turn. No matter how cold the air gets, ice will not normally form on the surface until the water is thoroughly mixed, and is pretty uniformly cool at all depths. Because of the mixing process, it is also pretty uniformly oxygenated. During the winter, trout drastically cut down on their feeding, or stop feeding altogether; as their rate of metabolism drops, their need for oxygen declines as well.

As soon as the ice starts breaking up in the spring, the trout make for the surface and the shallows. The surface water, although still quite cool, is a little warmer than that of the depths, and the first insects of the year provide a welcome change from winter fasting. However, as the year progresses, the surface gradually warms up. This time there is little mixing: the warm water stays on top, and the cooler water remains below. When the surface gets too warm for comfort, the trout go deeper to seek cooler water. How deep they can safely go will depend, among other things, on how big the lake is. If water is undisturbed, the dissolved gases it contains, including oxygen, will gradually seep out into the air, but the bigger the lake, the more subject it is to the effects of the wind, and the churning effect of a fairly stiff wind whipping up whitecaps on a really big lake is enough to replace, or more than replace, the oxygen lost by this seepage. On the other hand, the smaller the lake, the more protected it usually is from the wind, and in the absence of enough surface turbulence to replenish the oxygen supply, or of enough heavily-oxygenated water brought in by streams, the amount of dissolved oxygen in the water will gradually decline as the summer progresses, with the greatest incidence of oxygen starvation occurring at the greatest depths. Diagnosis: In the case of the particular lake under discussion, there are two places where trout are likely to be, if they are in the lake at all: they will be found either at the mouths of the streams, where at least some cool, oxygenated water is entering the lake, or at the **thermocline**, the point at which the water is deep enough to keep the trout cool, but not so deep as to deprive them of needed oxygen.

Of course, finding them is the hard part. Here is one way it might be done from a boat:

a. First off, fish just off the mouths of the streams. It is mid-summer, and the streams are low, but you can never be sure till you try. A stream sometimes is a better source of food and cool, highly-oxygenated water than it might at first appear.

b. If the streams produce, fine. If not, start bottom-fishing at a point along the shore, and gradually fish deeper and deeper until you have either connected or reached the deepest point in the lake.

If you connect, measure the depth carefully. As long as the spot continues to yield, stay there, but if the action stops, move to another spot at the same depth. To find another spot at the same depth, move the boat to deeper water, let out a weight on a line to the depth at which you have been successful, and direct the boat toward another point along the shore until your weight bumps bottom. Move the boat *very slowly*, otherwise the weight will trail behind the boat, and you will wind up fishing in water much shallower than that in which you were previously successful. (It doesn't hurt to check the depth again after the boat has stopped, and you can get a truly vertical reading.)

If you fail to connect, go through the same procedure several times, always starting out at a different point along the shore. If you have gone through the ceremony half a dozen times, and still haven't connected, this means: (1) There are no trout in the lake, because the conditions for trout survival–appropriate food, appropriate spawning grounds, water sufficiently cool and sufficiently oxygenated, a low level of pollution–have not been met. (2) There are trout in the lake, all right, but they are not feeding, largely because of excessively high temperatures. (3) There are trout in the lake, and the temperature is not too high, but they are not biting because it is too early in the day, it is too late in the day, it is too windy, it isn't windy enough, it is too cloudy, it isn't cloudy enough, the atmospheric pressure is too high or too low, the boat is the wrong color, you didn't spit on the bait three times, the rod is bewitched, Fate has it in for you, and so on.

From all this, I hope it is clear that fishing is not a science but an art, and an expert is not a person who will invariably come up with the right answer, but merely a person who has reduced his margin of error to manageable proportions.

Thus far we have considered some of the factors that induce fish to strike at bait or lures. It is also useful to know something about what happens if and when they do.

For most fish, most of the time, the process is simple

enough: either the fish comes near the bait or the bait comes near the fish; the fish interprets it as something edible, and he swallows it—or tries to. However, in some cases, the process is more elaborate.

When people fish for marlin in the West Indies, they usually go out in launches equipped with all kinds of special equipment: there is usually what looks like a barber chair bolted to the afterdeck; the massive rods are fitted with broad belts that allow the fisherman to transfer some of the strain from his arms to the rest of his body; and the boat is fitted with trolling spars (usually two, sprouting from the corners of the stern) terminating in a sort of seagoing clothespin. The line extends from the rod-tip to one of the clothespins (where it is gently but firmly gripped) to the lure in the water; when a fish strikes, the force of the strike pulls the line free of the clothespin, and the man holding the rod is fast to the fish.

The use of all this fancy equipment might lead the casual observer to conclude that without it you are not going to catch any marlin. But the Old Man, in Hemingway's *The Old Man and the Sea*, managed to catch an enormous one, despite the fact that he couldn't afford all that paraphernalia. All he had was a wooden skiff—sort of like an overgrown rowboat—fitted with a small, demountable sail; instead of the heavy trolling-rods, he had four green sticks fastened to the gunwale, to which were loosely hitched handlines, "as thick as a big pencil," terminating in big hooks at 40, 75, 100, and 125 fathoms. A bait fish was solidly stitched, head downward, onto each hook so that the shank of the hook was inside the fish and only the point protruded; on this point, a number of sardines were impaled through the eye-sockets. (The sticks were not meant to be used as rods—their only purpose was to indicate if a fish was working on any of the baits.) With this simple equipment, presenting the bait in a flagrantly unnatural manner, he was not trolling but simply drifting with the current.

The way the big marlin took the bait was as intricate as a ballet.

When the stick holding up the 100-fathom line dipped, the Old Man slipped the line off the stick and held it lightly between his fingers, diagnosing what the fish was doing by feel. He could tell that a marlin was pulling the sardines off the tip of the hook and eating them. When the sardines were eaten, the line started paying out; by the feel he knew that the fish was a big one and that he had taken the primary bait-fish sideways in his mouth and was moving off with it. If I read Hemingway correctly, the Old Man let him make off with at least 40 additional fathoms of line before he determined that the fish had turned and swallowed the bait. He then pulled back on the line as hard as he could, and had the fish fast.

Why did he have to let the fish run off at least 240 feet before he felt it was safe to set the hook? It's quite a story.

Fish which can easily bite off chunks of things–fish like sharks and the piranha of the Amazon–are relatively rare; most fish either laboriously haggle off ragged chunks of whatever it is they are feeding on or swallow their prey whole. Even a barracuda, popularly (but inaccurately) believed to operate much like a shark, cannot bite off anything with the wicked array of teeth he has; barracuda teeth serve only as anti-skid devices to prevent the bait-fish, once caught, from wriggling loose.

Perhaps the difficulties facing a game fish attempting to swallow a bait-fish whole can be better understood if we imagine a man in a pie-eating contest (no hands allowed), the pie desperately trying to escape, and the rules requiring that the pie be swallowed whole. Like the game fish, he would somehow have to seize the quarry in his mouth, be sure it is not going to get away, and then, by a deft movement of head and body, flip it into position to be swallowed.

Variations on this three-phase manoeuvre–(a) strike, (b) run, (c) turn and swallow–are played by many different game fish. However, the sequence usually doesn't work when artificials are used, simply because most artificials are so made that either the fish gets hooked as soon as he strikes or he doesn't get hooked at all.

Most of the time, game fish won't strike at an artificial unless it is moving, but there are some curious exceptions, precisely in those cases in which lack of motion fits the feeding pattern of the particular fish at the moment of the strike:

a. An old fishing buddy of mine once told me he was preparing to go trolling in a motor launch with no other company than a little boy. He had not got very far from shore, and was busy fiddling with the motor controls, when he noticed the boy, his mouth open and his eyes bugging out, wordlessly pointing sternward. What had happened was that his rod was rigged, ready to go; the feather-duster lure on the end of the line was bouncing around in the vessel's turbulent wake; and a swordfish was whacking at it with his "sword." Deducing that the swordfish thought the lure was alive, and was trying to kill it, the O.F.B. (Old Fishing Buddy) simply released the brake on his reel, and the lure stopped where it was and floated. Sure enough, the swordfish, now satisfied that the lure was dead, made a big turn, chomped down on the lure, and the fight was on.

b. Most commercial tuna boats nowadays use nets, but it wasn't too long ago that a typical commercial West-Coast tuna operation consisted of a big power boat of some kind and a bunch of muscular characters armed with oversized cane poles. Each pole was provided with a stout line terminating in a sizeable barbless hook more or less concealed in a bunch of chicken feathers.

As the boat chugged along, it left behind a trail of **chum**–chopped-up fish or squid. Tuna invariably travel in schools, and when they surface (following the trail of chum) they surface all at once, and don't stick around very long, so it behooves everybody on board to look sharp.

As soon as the school surfaced, the boat would stop, and everybody would whack his bunch of chicken feathers into the water. Tuna feed with desperate speed, as if they were starving to death; in their hurry, they apparently mistake the whitish blobs of feathers for particularly large and juicy chunks of the chum they have been gobbling up. Whenever a fish struck, the fisherman would heave mightily on the pole and swing the tuna over his shoulder and onto the deck; the barbless hook would bounce loose; and he would immediately whip the lure back into the water. With luck, he could heave three or four tuna onto the deck before the whole school would sound all at once. When that happened, the boat would resume cruising and dropping chum, looking for another school.

11. Fishing Techniques

Discounting oddities, such as "guddling"–the technique, favored by Scottish highlanders, of reaching shoulder-deep into the waters of a convenient "burn" (which is what the Scots persist in calling the small streams of their native land), locating a trout by feel, and hand-flipping him out onto the bank–there are five primary approaches to sports fishing: still-fishing, jigging, lobbing, trolling, and drifting.

"Lobbing" is not a standard fishing term. The dictionary says that "cast" means "to throw out (a fly, etc.) at the end of a fishing line," but dictionaries have the habit of lagging forty or fifty years behind the times, and since a casting rod is now only one of several contraptions for tossing out bait or lures, I feel that there is a need for a word to cover "getting the bait out there, no matter what kind of rod you are using."

1. **Still-Fishing** consists of putting a bait or lure into the water and leaving it there until a fish takes it. Since, as we have seen, most artificial lures don't appeal to fish unless they are drawn through the water fast enough to give them the action that makes them effective, most still-fishing is done with bait, either alive, in which case the action of the minnow, grasshopper, or what not adds motion to whatever other appeal the bait might have, or dead, in which case the bait has to depend largely on its taste/odor and its physical appearance.

An angler can engage in still-fishing dry-shod (from the shore, a bridge over a stream, and the like), standing in the water, as when the slope of a beach into the sea is too gradual to allow for effective surf-fishing from the shore, or from a boat. Each of these methods has its own appeal, but use of a boat will enormously increase the amount of fishing area that can be effectively explored. A fisherman is something like a traveling salesman–the more territory he can effectively cover, the more profitable contacts he can make.

A dryshod fisherman with a cane pole is restricted to a band of water twelve or fifteen feet wide, between the shore and the extreme limit of his line; a fisherman armed with a rod provided with any of the several kinds of reel can extend this distance as far as his rod can toss the bait; a fisherman in waders or hip boots can extend the distance still farther by as far as he can wade into the water

and still wield the rod; but a fisherman in a boat can fish
anywhere on the body of water in question that his boat
will take him.

A boat has yet another advantage. A still-fisherman in a boat can
always fish the area directly under-
neath the boat, which means that,
regardless of how the tackle is
rigged, and regardless of the direction in which the fish starts to stroll
off with the bait, there is always relatively little slack in the line
between the fish's mouth and the
end of the rod, and so the fisherman, simply by lifting his rod, can
immediately apply tension to the
line and (with luck) set the hook.

The fisherman on shore is much
more limited. He can insure that
there will be relatively little slack in the line between the
fish's mouth and the end of the rod only if his line enters
the water vertically, which is possible only if he confines
his efforts to an extremely narrow strip of shoreline. As
soon as he tosses his bait beyond the reach of his rod-tip,
the straight-line distance between rod-tip and bait will
start deviating from the vertical, and the farther out he
tosses the bait, the more closely the straight-line distance
between rod-tip and bait will deviate from the vertical and
approach the horizontal. If a fish takes the bait with the
line in this position, and moves off with it in any direction
except directly away from the fisherman, the fisherman's
ability to do anything decisive about it will either be
impaired or frustrated completely. For purposes of illustration, let us assume that the fish has taken the bait, and
is moving off with it *toward* the fisherman:

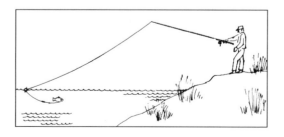

No matter how sharply he whips up his rod, the force of the tension exerted will be dissipated, serving only to take up some of the slack in the line (but not enough to do any good) and possibly alarm the fish so he drops the bait.

Perhaps a word of explanation about this "setting the hook" business might be in order.

A lot of people are positive that if you don't set the hook, you will never catch the fish, while others are equally certain that setting the hook is a lot of nonsense, because the fish will set it himself. There are at least two reasons I can think of why this failure to agree exists:

a. A hook cannot be set unless the line (and leader, if any) is taut between fish and rod-tip, and this, as we have seen, is not always the case, so it is easy to see how a fisherman who has vainly gone through the hook-setting motions a few dozen times can wind up believing that setting the hook is an idea whose time has not come.

b. Some fish swallow the bait, hook and all, so unhesitatingly that as soon as the fisherman feels a tug on the line, the fish is already firmly hooked. If the fish concerned is an impressive trophy, the fisherman may not object, but if it is a midget bullhead, all mouth and whiskers, he may not be so pleased. Infant bullheads are capable of swallowing quite large hooks, and usually the only way to get your hook back is to disassemble the bullhead.

It is therefore evident that the need for hook-setting, like almost everything else in angling, will depend on circumstances: for a dry-fly fisherman it is imperative and ever-present, but for a river-dweller setting a trot-line for catfish–forget it.

For one who has derived so much pleasure from fishing from the shores of unimpressive bodies of water, catching inconsiderable numbers of non-prestige fish of negligible size, it may seem ungrateful of me to keep harping on the limitations on still-fishing from the shore, but candor compels me to admit that I have not yet enumerated all the drawbacks associated with that mode of operation.

If you are going to toss a bait any distance at all, you will either have to do it with a fly rod, or use some kind of weight. (There are those who regard using a fly rod for still-fishing as sacrilege, but for natural presentation of a worm, it is hard to beat.) Using any other kind of rod (spinning or casting, for instance) you can use a float:

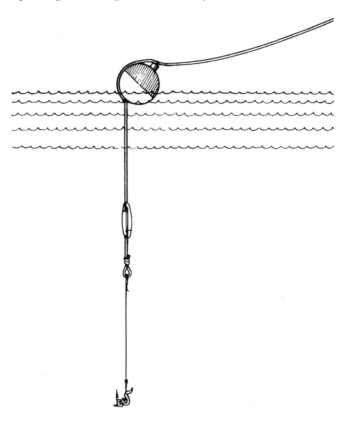

The conventional cork, plastic, or quill float has the advantage of letting you know when your bait has aroused interest, but it may be so lightweight that you may have to add a sizeable sinker to the line in order to get it out there any distance at all. This difficulty can be reduced somewhat by substituting a transparent plastic bubble for the conventional float. These are made so you can fill them with water, so if you put in enough water to provide enough throwing weight, but leave enough air to insure that the bubble will continue to float, you can use a smaller sinker:

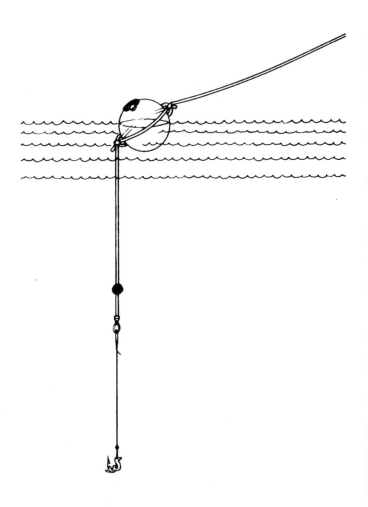

As an all-around general principle, it is a good idea never to use more sinker weight than you have to. If the water is absolutely still, you may be able to dispense with the sinker entirely, but if the water is moving, you may be obliged to pinch on one or more split-shot sinkers to keep the bait at the desired depth.

Or you can dispense with a float, keeping the line taut enough so you can keep track of what is going on by feel. This is what happens when you use the conventional arrangement of line, sinker, leader, and hook:

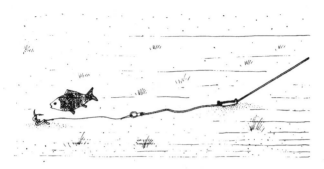

As soon as the fish starts to move off with the bait, he will feel the drag of the sinker–which must be sizeable, or you won't be able to throw it very far. To eliminate this unnatural situation, you can string the line through the eyelet of a pear-shaped sinker, clipping a split ring onto the line to prevent the sinker from sliding all the way down to the hook:

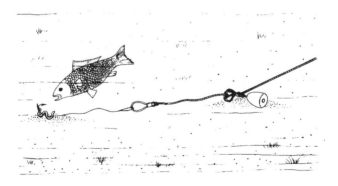

That way, when a fish starts to move off with the bait, the line will slide smoothly through the eyelet, and he will not feel much resistance; at the same time, the fisherman will be alerted by a gentle tug on the line.

Another way of alleviating the problem of weight drag is by clipping the split ring well *above* the weight, and using the leader as a dropper:

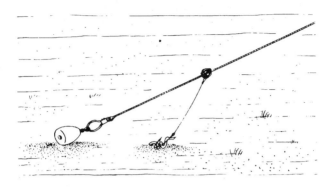

No matter which of these arrangements is used, they all require use of either a heavy or a bulky object, or both, which is bound to interfere with the control exerted by the fisherman on the fish, at least to some degree. This is particularly evident when the fish is hooked, and is bucketing all over the pool in his frantic attempts to escape. Ideally, the fisherman should maintain "a tight line"–enough tension to prevent the fish from gaining any more line than necessary, but not so much that the leader will break. This is hard to do if there is a sinker (and possibly a float as well) clanking around between the fish's jaw and the rod-tip, and the heavier the sinker, the more likely it is that the fish will break the leader and escape. Fame of a sort awaits the ingenious inventor who comes up with a device which, after being used to toss a bait into a likely-looking pool, will conveniently vanish.

Some of the commoner shapes for conventional lead sinkers are split-shot, in various sizes (which are pinched onto the line with pliers, or, in desperate cases, teeth), spindle-shaped ones, usually provided with a clamp-ring on each end, into which the line can be wedged, and pear-shaped ones, which can be hung onto loops or snap-rings:

Because of their density in relation to their size, sinkers have the annoying habit of getting lines and leaders hung up on underwater snags. You can sometimes buy relatively snagless lead sinkers; they are shaped like wobbling spoons without hooks, and when retrieved, instead of trying to drape the line and leader around every snag on the bottom, will flutter safely over most underwater obstacles. However, if you cut the handles from ordinary household spoons (teaspoons for spinning rods, tablespoons for casting rods) and drill a hole at the tip end, they will work just as well:

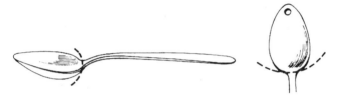

There is also a type of sinker widely used for salt-water still-fishing. It is in the shape of an upside-down pyramid, with an eyelet cast into the middle of its top (flat) side, so it can conveniently be hung onto a line:

This type of sinker exemplifies the fact that, although a newcomer moving into strange territory can learn a lot about how to fish the local waters by observing and imitating the natives, if he imitates them *too* slavishly, he risks inheriting the shortcomings, as well as the advantages, of the methods they use. It works like this:

One of the ways for rigging up a line for still-fishing in salt water is to hang one of these pyramidal sinkers onto

the end of the line, and, a little higher up, fasten on a
spreader, a simple wire yoke, from which dangle hooks
on short leaders:

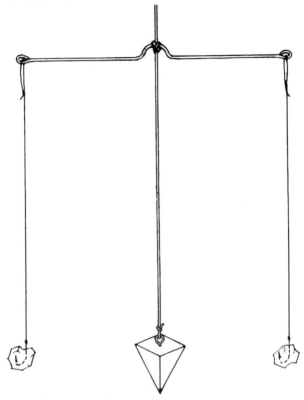

The point of the sinker digs into the sand or gravel, holding the bait still enough so that, despite the ebb and flow
of the surf, foraging fish can get a good look at it, and the
spreader keeps the leaders from getting tangled up in the
line. This rig is widely used for catching all sorts of bot-
tom-feeding fish, including flounder. Well, most fish keep
moving, swiftly or sluggishly, depending on variety, as
they feed, but the flounder doesn't–he simply lies there,
pretending to be part of the sea bottom, and waits for
food to come to him. For this reason, the best kind of
sinker to use for flounder is not the pyramidal kind, but
one with a round bottom, so the rig will wander around
in the surf more, and presumably come within reach of
more flounder.

2. **Jigging**, like still-fishing, maintains the bait more or less in the same spot, but adds interest to whatever is being offered by jiggling it up and down. This can be done either with a jig, an artificial lure made especially for the purpose, or just about any kind of bait. Jigging was probably invented in connection with ice fishing: if you are bottom-fishing through a hole in the ice, and the water is forty feet deep, up and down is the only dimension in which you can impart motion to a lure or bait.

It is to be noted that, whereas still-fishing practically never involves artificial lures, jigging can and sometimes does, one more illustration of the fact that if an artificial lure does not move, it becomes meaningless, and perhaps effectively invisible, to fish.

It is possible to jig with a natural bait which at the same time acts as an artificial lure. When the ice fishermen on Lake Champlain are jigging for smelt, one of the commonest baits used is a thin, narrow slice of the same fish they are angling for. A heavy sinker is tied on the end of the line, a leader and hook are clipped on as a dropper, and the point of the hook is run through one end of a slice of smelt, roughly the size and shape of a small minnow. Since the sinker is heavy and the dropper light, the motion imparted to the bait by jigging produces a fairly good imitation of an erratically swimming minnow.

Dry flies can be manipulated by "dapping"–a process something like jigging, except that it is done on the surface, rather than under water. The method is very old–Izaak Walton mentions it, claiming that it works best "on the evening of a hot day." The angler finds a pool, preferably surrounded by brush; crouching low on the ground to avoid being seen, he then pokes the end of his rod through the shrubbery and lets out just enough line to allow the fly to light on the water. By alternately raising and lowering the rod-tip, he makes the fly look like an insect that has fallen into the water and is vainly attempting to fly away.

3. **Lobbing** consists of tossing out a lure or bait with the intent of imparting to it motion of interest to fish. In stream fishing with flies, the motion is normally imparted by the current moving the fly along, either on the surface or beneath it; for most other kinds of fishing, the motion is provided by cranking the reel handle and retrieving the lure or bait.

As with still-fishing, if the lure is too light to toss out very far, you will have to add weight, either floating or sinking. A spinning rod rigged with a water-filled floating bubble works well for panfish. (I have been assured that it also works for trout, but I have yet to be convinced.) Tie on the bubble about eighteen inches above the end of the line, where you hang on a small sinker–just heavy enough to keep the lure well under water. At the same point, hang on an eighteen-inch leader with either a small fly or the smallest possible wobbling spoon. Retrieve *very slowly*:

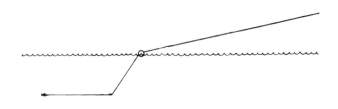

Still-fishing with bait and lobbing bait do not work the same way at all. The same fish which, when you are still-fishing, will refuse to touch the bait unless it is a miracle of natural presentation, will sometimes make a frantic grab at the same kind of bait being towed in the wake of an improbable assemblage of hardware. This would seem to imply that the thing to do is to forget about still-fishing and concentrate on lobbing out bait hung onto improbable assemblages of hardware. Unfortunately, it doesn't work that way. The key word is "sometimes"; if you try one method, and it doesn't work, you don't argue with the fish–you try something else.

One of the advantages of lobbing is that it allows you to cover the fishing area pretty thoroughly in a relatively short time. If you are lobbing from the shore, you can pick a spot and toss-and-retrieve all over a fan-shaped area; if nothing happens, you can move a few yards farther along and do it all over again. If you are lobbing from a boat, you can move the boat from place to place, halting at places that look promising, and work the area thoroughly before moving on. Or you can drift (or be paddled) parallel to the shoreline, lobbing and retrieving as you go.

One of the drawbacks to lobbing is that it tends to give you a false sense of accomplishment. It is a common human failing to judge the value of an enterprise in terms of the energy expended on it, so I suppose it is reasonable to expect that an angler who has been conscientiously flailing the water all day without a strike will take a cheerier view of the matter than a still-fisherman who has been crouching over his rod all day without a nibble, although the results have been the same in either case.

Here are what I believe to be some of the commoner faults that bait- or lure-tossing fishermen can commit:

a. **Failure to Vary the Lure.** Although it seems obvious that, if one kind of lure doesn't work, the thing to do is try another, I suspect that there are fishermen who fall so deeply in love with one kind of lure that they will fish all day with it, and then wonder why "they aren't biting." Much more numerous are the fishermen who vary the lure, all right, but don't pay much attention to what is replacing what else. If you change a medium-sized light-colored surface lure for another medium-sized light-colored surface lure, you are less likely to hit on a winning combination than if your replacement is small rather than medium-sized, dark-colored rather than light-colored, or deep-running rather than working on the surface.

b. **Retrieving at Improper Speed.** For freshwater fishing, this usually means retrieving too fast. This does not mean that a bass or a pike cannot put on an impressive burst of speed if he feels like it–it simply means that if the speed at which the bait or lure is retrieved is considerably in excess of the cruising speed at which the fish being sought normally operates, your strikes will be few.

c. **Defective Strategy.** Suppose you find a likely-looking weed-bed, in which you suspect pickerel to be lurking. Let us say for the sake of argument that the weed-bed extends north and south along the shore; you maneuver your boat to the west of it, and lob your lure at the weed-bed from that direction.

A much more effective strategy would be to station your boat at the north or south end, lob the lure as close as possible to the weed-bed, and retrieve parallel to it. This has several advantages: (1) As every artilleryman knows, it is much easier to achieve accuracy in traverse (direction) than in elevation (range), so you can drop your lure much closer to the weed-bed if you lob from the north or south, rather than from the west. (2) If there are several pickerel in the weed-bed, and you lob from the west, whether your lure lands close to the pickerel or not will depend purely on chance, whereas if you lob from the north or south, you will inevitably parade the lure reasonably close to all of them. (3) If you lob from the west, all the pickerel will realize is that something has fallen into the water and then swum off before he can get a good look at it, whereas if you lob from the north or south, the pickerel can see the lure coming, wait until it is good and close, and then pounce.

4. **Trolling** consists of trailing a bait or lure behind a moving boat. This can be done at various speeds; it can be done either by muscle-power, as with oars or a paddle, or by means of a motor; it can be done at various depths; and it can be done with the assistance of various techniques.

a. **Speed.** Trolling too slow is usually less serious than trolling too fast. A game fish of a particular species might be reluctant to strike at a bait or lure that is moving much more slowly than its normal prey, but no fish can possibly strike at a bait or lure exceeding its own top speed. It is therefore evident that although trolling too slow might lessen the likelihood of a strike, trolling too fast may make a strike impossible.

The speed with which a particular bait or lure should be trolled will vary in response to two considerations: the type of fish sought, and the limitations of the lure used.

(1) **The Type of Fish Sought.** If you are surface-trolling in the Gulf of Mexico for Spanish mackerel, you don't have to worry about trolling too fast, because the chances are the mackerel can easily swim faster than your boat can move. If you are trolling the channels off Cuttyhunk for striped bass, a more moderately-paced fish, your speed should be less. (To know how much less, watch the charter boats.) If you are trolling for yellow perch in a small lake, mooch along as slowly as possible.

(2) **Limitations of the Lure Used.** As we have seen in Chapter 8, the action of many of them, especially plugs and wobbling spoons, is a factor of their speed, and if trolled too fast or too slow, they will not work; moreover,

the range of speed that will work varies widely between one lure and another. If a fisherman intends to use such a lure, he ought first to insure that the lure to be used is appropriate to the fish being sought (either by asking other people whose pronouncements seem reasonable or on the basis of his own experience), and then take care to troll within the speed limits of the lure in question.

Bait, not being provided with special planing surfaces to provide it with a specific type of action, is less sensitive. So are spinners. Since a spinner is merely an assemblage of hardware that involves a shiny element which, revolving when pulled through the water, will sparkle, it will work at just about any speed. And since imparting motion to a bait seems to remove a good deal of the need for presenting it naturally, even for fairly wary fish, supplementing whatever appeal a bait may have by trailing it behind a spinner seldom does harm, and may do a lot of good. (It tends to twist the line, though–see Chapter 8.)

One kind of saltwater bait that has long been popular worldwide is a dead but still fresh fish, rigged so as to give the illusion of being alive by the simple device of being pulled through the water head first. There are many ways of rigging whole fish, some of them very elaborate, but one of the simpler ways is to pass the hook and line in at the mouth, out one of the gill-slits, and around the body, and then anchor the hook firmly in the tail:

It may be necessary to sew the lips of the bait fish together, to prevent the mouth from scooping water and providing a less than ideal type of action.

b. **Muscle Power or Motor.** Using muscle power rather than horsepower to troll with has certain advantages, not the least of which is that the speeds attained tend to be closer to the ideal, especially for freshwater fishing. Rowboats and john boats have an advantage over canoes in that the oarsman faces the stern, and hence can more easily keep an eye on his line. A Japanese friend of mine told me that as a boy he did a lot of fishing in a boat fitted with a sweep at the stern, instead of conventional oars–it worked fine, he said. A project to be carried out by one of those rare individuals who aren't already swamped with more projects than they can handle would be to rig up a boat with a stern-facing seat and a pair of foot pedals to operate a sculling rudder–that way, the fisherman could keep an eye on the line as well as a rower can, and at the same time have both hands free.

And then there are the pleasures and pains that go with motors.

Once upon a time, all boat motors were inboard motors, because nobody had got around to inventing the other kind yet. They were usually located amidships, and provided thrust to the propeller by means of a long shaft, extending sternward and downward through a mysterious arrangement known as a stuffing box, which wasn't supposed to leak but sometimes did.

When outboard motors came along, they eliminated the problem of the stuffing-box, but shifted the weight of the motor from amidships to the stern, so you sometimes had to stack a few cinderblocks in the bow to keep the boat on a reasonably even keel.

For quite a while, one of the problems connected with trolling with outboard motors was based on the fact that every time you tried to throttle the motor down slow enough to troll with, the motor would quit. When this happened you would get yourself a monstrosity known as a cavitation plate, and clamp it onto the propeller. Its purpose was to deflect some of the thrust of the propeller blades, and hence allow the boat to operate at slower speeds. It did, but it also made it almost impossible for you to steer the boat even approximately in the direction you wanted it to go, so you would then take off the cavitation plate and hurl it into the swamp.

Outboard motors are a little more sophisticated than they used to be, and they throttle down better than they used to, but I notice that you can still find boats with two motors clamped on their transoms–a powerful one, to get you where you want to go in a hurry, and a low-powered one, to troll with.

c. **Depth.** You can troll on the surface; you can troll at an intermediate depth; you can troll on the bottom. Except for a very short period in spring, and an even shorter period in late fall, if you are trolling for lake trout or land-locked salmon, you are either trolling on the bottom or you are not catching much. The only way you can be sure you are trolling on the bottom is to feel the bait or lure bumping along the bottom.

A fellow on Vancouver Island once told me that there was a time when fishermen desirous of trolling the deep channels with which the region abounds would use discarded automobile batteries as trolling sinkers. A few feet ahead of the lure, they would fasten on the battery with a breakaway hitch, so that if a fish gave evidence of having been hooked, a quick tug on the line would release the hitch, the battery would sink to the bottom, and the fisherman would play the fish directly. It eventually occurred to the community that, aside from the fact that battery acid is tough on living organisms, if people kept doing this long enough, the channels would eventually fill up with old batteries, and so the practice was discontinued.

There are patented planing devices which, like the batteries, are used to force the bait or lure to the bottom, and can be deactivated by a sharp tug on the line; however, instead of falling free of the line, they simply fold up so they offer only negligible resistance to the thrust of the water. The use of lines in which the eight of the line itself obviates the need for a sinker or planing device is now common. You have to be careful with weighted lines of this type–they will kink if you bend them too sharply, but they are otherwise satisfactory.

d. **Techniques.** It sometimes happens that a fisherman who has been trolling unsuccessfully for a while is about to quit for the day, but just as he is turning the boat around to go back home, he gets a strike. This happens so often it cannot be coincidence, or just the perversity of fate. It may be that a fish has been following the lure for quite a while, but had not struck until the lure had made a sudden turn, as if to escape. Or perhaps the fact that the boat made a sharp turn allowed the lure to sink to a deeper level, where the fish happened to be. When a boat towing a lure makes a turn, the lure does not follow the boat in track; it makes a turn whose radius of arc is much greater than that of the boat. When this happens, the tension on the line lessens for the duration of the turn, and the lure sinks lower in the water. The fisherman can exploit this phenomenon by working a number of 90° turns into his trolling pattern. It also does no harm to note the location and approximate depth of the lure when you get a strike, and troll past the same point again; where there was one, there may be more.

For deep trolling, a somewhat different technique is required. If you want to troll the channels, you will presumably cover more fishable water if you follow the line of a particular channel than if you troll at right angles to it, and hence knowing where the channels are makes your coverage of the area more effective than if you troll at random. It is usually difficult to find a chart of a fresh-water lake, especially if it is of no great size, but anybody fishing a part of the seacoast with any pretensions to navigation should have no difficulty getting hold of harbor charts, which show depth patterns in considerable detail. By plotting the location and orientation of the primary channels in relation to prominent landmarks, you can fish the area much more efficiently than might otherwise be the case.

5. **Drifting** is like trolling, except that, instead of using either muscle-power or a motor to impart motion to the boat (and hence to the bait or lure) movement is provided by such natural forces as wind, the current, or tide. This is a much-neglected method of angling, possibly because it looks so aimless. A fisherman who put-puts by in a motorboat, one hand on the tiller and the other clutching a rod bend double by the force of the water, looks purposeful; by contrast, a couple of characters in a boat, lolling back in their seats as the boat drifts along, might well be mistaken for still-fishermen who are unaware that their anchor-rope has parted.

However, drifting has certain built-in advantages: Since the force of the wind is seldom constant, even if it keeps blowing in the same direction, this frequently imparts to the bait or lure a hesitant, erratic quality of considerable appeal to fish, and the fisherman doesn't have to divide his attention between fishing and navigation.

If left to its own devices, the boat will keep slewing around as the wind, current, or tide drives it along. To prevent this, you can use a sea anchor. A sea anchor looks very much like one of those wind socks used on small airfields; to a stiffener ring is attached a cloth tube in the shape of a cone with the tip chopped off:

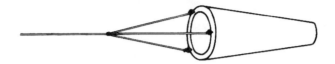

Because of the denser medium through which it moves, it must be made of sturdier material than the lightweight synthetics used to make wind socks–canvas or heavy duck. If a sea anchor is fastened to the bow and stern of a small boat with two lines of equal length, it will maintain the boat broadside to the wind:

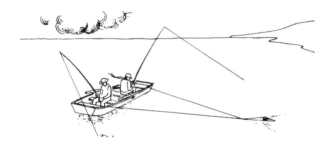

12. Boats

There once was a fellow named Walt Kelly, who used to draw a cartoon featuring a possum named Pogo and his friends–Albert the alligator, Howlan' Owl, Churchy La Femme, Rackety Coon Chile, and a whole passel of others, who lived in the Okefenokee Swamp. Once in a while they would angle for brim-fish, which is Pogo talk for bream, which is one of several confusing ways you can refer to sunfish. When they did, they would use a scow.

Walt could draw a scow so you could not only see what it looked like, but also be reasonably sure of how it had been made. To make a Pogo-type scow, you get a pair of heavy planks, cut cattywampus wedges off the corners of one edge, and stand them, parallel to each other, on the other edge. You then nail on smaller planks crosswise, with big ole nails, clap on slightly wider planks for end-pieces, and you have yourself a boat of sorts. Turned right-side-up, and provided with such amenities as oarlocks and cross-planks for seats, it looks like this:

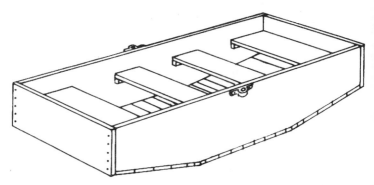

By fitting the bottom cross-planks together very tightly, and keeping the boat underwater long enough for the wood to swell, you can probably prevent serious leaks. For non-serious leaks, you can either gunk up the seams with road tar or get used to the idea of water sloshing around your ankles.

The beauty of a scow like this is that almost anybody can build one. However, it is admittedly a pretty clumsy proposition. By altering the basic building line only slightly–cutting the sides of the bottom panel you are going to substitute for bottom cross-planks slightly convex instead of straight, and cutting the sides and end-pieces so that the plan view of the boat will be bigger at the gunwale

126

than at the bottom–and using different materials–like marine plywood for the sides and bottom, and screws instead of nails–you will produce what is nowadays referred to as a john boat:

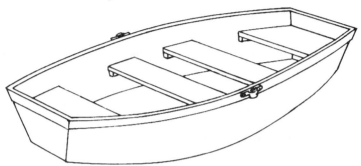

The fact that the process of making a john boat is easy to describe does not necessarily mean that building one is easy.

One of the advantages of a john boat may be summed up in the cryptic phrase, "the more it sinks, the less it sinks." Because the freeboard is upward-sloping rather than vertical, if the first hundred pounds you load into it makes it ride on the water an inch deeper, every additional hundred pounds will make it ride a progressively smaller fraction of an inch deeper still. At the same time, because of this same sloping freeboard, a well-built john boat tends to rise under the waves rather than plowing through them, so you don't ship much water. With a medium-power outboard motor hung on it, it makes a very satisfactory all-purpose boat.

If you built a boat more or less like a john boat, but made one end pointy instead of square, you would wind up with a variant of the common or garden-variety rowboat:

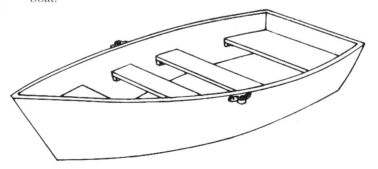

Personally, I have never seen the advantage of the rowboat over the john boat: it reduces available space, provides less flotation for the same length, and, in rough weather, tends to throw water all over whoever is riding in the bow. Perhaps the rowboat was originally designed on false analogy with big ships, which had to have deep, well-ballasted holds to counterbalance the thrust of the wind against what looked like several acres of sails, and hence either had to have well-designed underwater streamlining (including a pointy bow) or put up with slow speeds.

Or perhaps it wasn't–with all the prams, dinghies, dories, and what not there are, it's hard to tell, and I'm not an expert. Anyway, for my money, although the john boat is pretty good, the best all-around small boat for fishing is a canoe.

A canoe is not too expensive; if made of modern materials, it will last a long time with minimum maintenance; it is not difficult to learn how to manipulate. It is also reasonably safe. Of course, anybody who plans to spend time in an open boat should either know how to swim or get used to wearing a life jacket a lot, but, provided with watertight buoyant chambers or blocks of plastic flotation material, a modern canoe is practically unsinkable.

Best of all, it is very light-weight. We Americans have not yet got over our admiration for sheer size and superfluous horsepower, so for many people, "getting the boat into the water" is a pretty elaborate ritual. The family sedan, to which is attached a trailer bearing a launch surely big enough to cruise the West Indies for marlin, backs with painful slowness toward the launching ramp of the access area on a lake of quite moderate size; as the mighty vessel is slowly being nudged and cajoled into the water, you half expect a pretty girl to appear, call out, "I christen thee the *Queen Mary*," and smash a bottle of champagne over its bows.

A canoe can dispense with all that. It needs no trailer because it can with perfect security and considerable ease ride on a cartop rack, and any place along a lake or stream where the water is a few inches deep will do as a launching area.

The kind of cartop rack to get will depend on your temperament. If you are heavily committed to Togetherness, a simple double-crossbar type will do, but if you plan on doing any solitary fishing, you'd better get the type in which the front end rests on a single crossbar and the back end is held by a swivel-mounted clamp supported by the back bumper–with this kind, you can unload the canoe all by yourself.

The very first canoes, as we all know, were made of birch-bark, and then for quite a while were made of doped canvas, but nowadays most of them are either fiberglass, aluminum, or some kind of cast plastic. (Grumman Aircraft originally manufactured aluminum canoes as part of a joint Government/industry program to cushion the blow of massive layoffs of aircraft workers at the end of World War II, but the line proved to be more profitable than anticipated, so they are still being sold.)

The fanciest and most expensive canoes are usually those made of fiberglass; aluminum canoes are usually somewhat cheaper. When you put a warm aluminum canoe into cool water, it tends to make funny noises, which may or may not bother you, as the metal suddenly contracts. Unless I am mistaken, the cheapest commercially-sold canoe you can buy just now is made of polyethylene or some other cast plastic. Don't depend on them to stay cheap, though–the primary ingredient in plastics is petroleum, and making plastics requires massive amounts of power, so cast plastic canoes may soon price themselves out of the market.

Well, and how about a motor? A canoe doesn't need much power to push it around, and the smallest possible outboard motor–about 2 HP,–is plenty big enough. Perhaps best of all is an electric motor, or "troller," as the Sears catalog persists in calling it. Trollers are lightweight, pretty reliable, relatively inexpensive, non-polluting, and quiet. Besides, they don't burn petroleum products. If you get one, you will also need a battery to run it and a plug-in battery-charger to revive its spirits after each use.

Mounting it is no problem. You can get canoes with squared-off sterns designed for use with motors, electric or otherwise, but standard canoes can also accommodate motors by means of a simple clamp-on adapter.

As long as you confine your fishing to small lakes and gentle streams, the canoe will do the job nicely, but if you are going to fish in fairly big lakes, turbulent rivers, or on the open sea, you may need a bigger and sturdier boat. Listing all the kinds of waters there are and the kind of boats that best fit them would take several volumes; however, the governing principle involved can be stated simply enough: the bigger the body of water fished in, and the greater the straight-line distance between the launching point and the most distant point to be reached in the course of the day's (or week's, or month's) fishing, the more attention must be paid to the seaworthiness of the boat used. This is simply another way of saying that the more likely you are to run into rough weather, and the farther away from home base you could be when a storm breaks, the more careful you have to be.

It is not only on the open sea that small boats can get in trouble–in a way, long, narrow big lakes are even more treacherous, partly because, until experience teaches him better, the newcomer finds it hard to believe that you can possibly get in trouble on anything with clearly visible shores, and partly because a shift of a few degrees in the direction of the wind can with horrid suddenness transform the tranquil surface into an expanse of savage white caps. The force of a wind that has decided to come roaring down the slot, with nothing to bar its progress for 50 or 100 miles, must be seen to be appreciated.

This is not to say that a small boat should never venture out on a big lake. If you make a habit of keeping posted on the latest 24-hour weather forecast in the area, if you keep your excursions short, if you stay fairly close to the shore (not just close enough to see the shore clearly –what looks like 200 yards sometimes turns out to be closer to two miles) and if you keep an eye to windward–the direction from which trouble will come if it comes at all–a canoe or small boat should be safe enough. But if you want to troll the deeps for lake trout or landlocked salmon, or go a few miles out in the Gulf of Mexico to see if you can scare up a few Spanish mackerel, get a bigger boat.

13. Conservation

Nowadays, almost everybody is aware that we should be concerned about world ecology. This is a relatively new concept; for most of history, if there was in nature an animal or plant that was useful to man, most people thought that the only thing to do about it was to exploit it for their own advantage–it never occurred to anybody that he ought to help improve its viability as a species, thereby preventing it from becoming extinct.

The passage of time eventually forced us to realize that, as world population increased, wild habitat shrank, and pollution of air and water increased both in volume and complexity. Unless man did something about it, an appallingly large number of useful animals and plants would indeed become extinct.

Once we became aware of the problem, we found it was more complicated than we had thought.

Rachel Carson, in her book *Silent Spring*, pointed out that if a farmer wanted to prevent insects from damaging his crop, the usual thing to do was to spray the plants with poison, thereby unleashing several unforeseen consequences. The poison would kill or disable a lot of the insects, some of which were washed into a nearby body of water, where they were snapped up by the resident fish; some of the fish were in turn snapped up by the resident waterfowl. In that way, poison intended to kill insects killed fish and waterfowl as well.

Farley Mowat, in his book *Never Cry Wolf*, recalls being surprised when an Eskimo told him, "The wolf keeps the caribou strong." Since the book was written, the idea that certain living creatures don't thrive unless they share living space with some sort of predator that keeps them from multiplying to the point of endangering their own food supply, or of becoming increasingly vulnerable to certain infectious diseases, has become an ecological commonplace.

And then we are told that each species must have a suitable habitat–that is, an area that is big enough to allow a certain amount of free movement, that provides it with enough food and water, and is not so heavily visited by man and other predators that it can be killed off faster than it can reproduce.

Again, this sort of thing turned out to be more compli-

131

cated than at first supposed. The whooping crane winters in a relatively small area in Texas, among the oil rigs, and breeds in a relatively small area in northern Canada. It, like many other birds, is territorial, and during the breeding season, the male of the brooding pair patrols an area of approximately four square miles, driving away any trespassing whooping crane that has had the temerity to set foot on what the breeding male considers his nesting area.

There is no law of nature that compels the whooping crane to behave in exactly this way–it is simply the complex of habits it happened to adopt in the course of its evolution. As a matter of fact, there is a creature–the sandhill crane–whose feeding and migrating habits do not differ much from those of the whooping crane, but because it is less fussy about the boundaries of its nesting and wintering areas, and is more tolerant of others of its kind in the vicinity of its nest, it has never spent time teetering on the edge of extinction, as the whooping crane has.

Once we started taking protection of the environment seriously, it became increasingly obvious that there is no point in categorizing all plants and animals as Useful (in which case they are to be protected) or Useless (in which case they may be allowed to drift into extinction). The relations between species are so intricate that it is extremely difficult, and in many cases impossible, to tell in advance what the effect of allowing any particular species to become extinct will be. Shoot all the coyotes, and you find yourself up to your knees in field mice. Eradicate what you regard as a noxious weed, and your favorite songbird disappears.

And so it has belatedly dawned upon us that the only way we can insure that damage to Spaceship Earth is kept to a minimum is to protect all species, the ugly and presumably useless as well as the handsome and undoubtedly useful.

How do fish make out in the survival sweepstakes?

First, the bad news.

It sometimes happens that a particular creature becomes extinct, and its extinction is mistakenly ascribed to the wrong cause. There are historical references to flying passenger pigeons as being "so numerous as to darken the sky," so when they became extinct in 1914, it was natural to suppose that their extinction was due to excessive harvesting pressures. It is true that they were slaughtered by the thousands, but it is likely that it was the loss of appropriate habitat, possibly chestnut forests, plus an inability to change their life patterns enough to cope with a new situation that got them in trouble.

Early in the 20th century, people at the St. Louis Zoo noticed that passenger pigeons were getting scarce, so they rounded up a small flock of them and installed them in a roomy zoo cage. Passenger pigeons were extremely gregarious, and it seems that the presence of several thousand individuals of its own kind was necessary to trigger mating and reproduction. When no additional passenger pigeons showed up at the St. Louis Zoo, the captive group apparently interpreted this as an indication that the breeding season had not yet arrived, and so they all died of old age without producing offspring.

Saltwater fish are indeed threatened by over-harvesting. Over time, Americans discovered that depending on wilderness as a primary source of animal protein, mostly in the form of bear and deer, was a lost cause, but they never got around to making the same decision in the case of sea fish. The sea has traditionally been regarded as so vast that over-exploitation of its animal-protein resources is impossible.

The sea is vast, but it is not infinite. The recent history of the fisheries industry has paralleled that of industry in general; in an attempt to expand their market share, or merely to remain viable, many companies have invested in bigger (and hence more expensive) boats and more sophisticated (and hence more expensive) equipment, such as sonar viewers to locate and exploit schools of fish more efficiently. This has been going on just when fish stocks worldwide have been shown to be in decline.

There isn't much government can do about a situation like this. It can extend tax benefits to commercial fishermen, but the dollar amount involved is unlikely to be great enough to solve the problem. It can refuse to license people desiring to enter the commercial-fishing business, but this is just another case of locking the stable door after the horse has been stolen. It can limit fishing seasons, or the size of the catch, knowing that this is likely to impose additional hardship on fisheries struggling to remain viable.

What is more, our government doesn't control the open sea–any control we can hope to impose must be worked out by treaty with other governments, notably Canada, which is as much interested in the Grand Banks of Newfoundland as we are.

And then there is Japan, which seems to have given new meaning to the expression "step up the pace of production." One of the devices used by the Japanese was what might be called "the endless trot-line." As a fishing boat was proceeding on an extensive circular course, a line, onto which at regular intervals were fastened short lengths of finer line terminating in baited hooks, was reeled into the water. When the boat had arrived at the point at which the first hook had been dropped, the crew could pick up the main line and reel it on board, where they could remove the fish that had been hooked while the boat was sailing on its circular course. If desired, as fish were removed from the hooks, the hooks could be re-baited, the line could be put back into the water, and another circular course begun.

How about freshwater fish?

In one way, they are better off than saltwater fish. As soon as a problem arises, a state regulatory agency can decree corrective measures (closing certain areas to fish-ing, reducing the legal catch, etc.) without loss of time. However, there is one area in which freshwater fish are much more vulnerable than saltwater fish: pollution.

When a seagoing oil tanker springs a leak, the damage may be extensive, but is limited to a given region. Freshwater pollution doesn't work like that. Relatively few bodies of fresh water are really large, and the thousands of lakes and streams of more moderate size run the risk, not only of being polluted, but of being wiped out. If water is clear and sparkling, this is often taken as evi-dence of its purity, but there are lakes in the United States that are clear and sparkling because they are sterile–few organisms can live in them.

In addition to saltwater fish (which will die if put into fresh water), and freshwater fish (which will die if put into salt water), there are anadromous fish, which have some-how figured out how to spend a part of their lives in salt water and a part in fresh water. They don't all do it the same way.

Common eels spawn in the Sargasso Sea (which is not really a sea, but merely an eddy in the Atlantic Ocean, where a lot of floating seaweed tends to pile up), where-upon their offspring make their way either to Europe or the United States, depending on where their parents came from, swim up through freshwater streams to bodies of fresh water, where they mature; when mature, they return to the Sargasso Sea, spawn, and die.

Salmon, on the other hand, spawn in the headwaters of many rivers, including those on both the Atlantic and Pacific coasts; when their offspring have achieved a cer-tain amount of growth, they make their way downstream until they reach the ocean, where they remain one or several years, feeding voraciously; after they mature, they return to the same headwater in which they spent a portion of their youth and spawn. There are several kinds of west-coast salmon, but only one kind of Atlantic salmon: west-coast salmon die after spawning, but some Atlantic salmon manage to stagger back to the ocean, where they can recuperate in preparation for another spawning run.

Eels are pretty tough, and seem to be getting along nicely despite threats to their well-being, but salmon are a different story.

When Lewis and Clark portaged around the rapids of what was later to be called Celilo Falls, on the Columbia River between Washington and Oregon, they found there a small tribe of Indians, the Wyampums, whose primary source of sustenance was the salmon that came through the rapids on their annual spawning run. Other tribes–Yakimas, Umatillas, Warm Springs and Nez Perce–also used the fisheries during the spawning season, but the Wyampums lived there the year round.

By virtue of the Middle Oregon Treaty, signed June 25, 1855, the Wyampums retained the right to continue fishing for salmon in the manner of their ancestors; they accordingly maintained a system of wooden platforms along the shore on which to stand and scoop out the salmon with dip-nets when the spring run was in progress.

Along about 1950, the government started work on a dam-building project, in the process of which the Falls would become part of the dam impoundment, thus putting the dip-net tribal fishing arrangement out of business. The Wyampums were moved out of their admittedly modest homes into houses even less pretentious, built by the Bureau of Indian Affairs, and the old village was bulldozed and burned. Compensation to the tribe consisted of a lump-sum payment of $3,750 per capita–not much return for the loss of an ample supply of first-class edible protein at very little overhead cost (platform, dip-nets, a little muscle power) for as long as the salmon kept coming up the river. In theory, the rules governing a treaty with an Indian tribe are essentially the same as those governing a treaty with any other foreign power, and may not be unilaterally abrogated except for cause, but the Wyampums had to move just the same. The chief, Tommy Kuni Thompson, refused to "signature his salmon away," and so got nothing at all, and eventually died in a nursing home as a welfare case.

So much for the bad news. Now for the good news.

Although the dispossession of the Wyampums took place only a few years ago, the story already sounds like ancient history, and it is hard to imagine a similar maneuver taking place today. Not so long ago, we used to think that any project going under the equivocal name of "development" and costing more than a million dollars must be allowed to go through, regardless of whose rights were violated, because development produces progress and progress creates wealth and wealth generates happiness. However, we seem to have had a sudden change of heart–with overpopulation and energy crises, we are beginning to realize that our natural resources, though considerable, are finite, and, unless we are careful, we may develop ourselves into a second Stone Age.

This new awareness has been accompanied by a considerably increased public interest in conservation. Not all fishermen get involved in conservation, but they all ought to be aware of some of the potentialities and limitations of conservation projects. A fairly good idea of the problems you can run into in connection with a conservation project involving fish can be obtained by study of the present movement to restore salmon fishing to the Eastern seaboard to something like its former splendor.

Atlantic salmon begin their lives as hatchlings in one of the cool freshwater streams of Europe or the East Coast of the United States. They develop from **alevins** (the newly-hatched phase) to **parr** (the freely-swimming and -feeding phase) and eventually, as **smolt** (the migratory phase) make their way down the stream to the ocean. They normally spend from two to four years in the ocean, feeding voraciously and attaining considerable size. When they mature, they seek out and ascend their native rivers, returning to spawn on the particular stretch of stream where they spent their extreme youth, starting up another cycle of salmon generation.

The mechanism whereby salmon can find their way back to their point of origin is quite similar to the way data is stored in a computer's "memory"–or perhaps it is more accurate to say that the way data is stored in a computer's "memory" is quite similar to the mechanism whereby salmon can find their way back to their point of origin–after all, the salmon were there first. When a salmon is still immature, his nervous system is somehow "imprinted" with the memory of the water in which he finds himself, so that he is "programmed" to return to that spot and no other.

Before our country was industrialized, Atlantic salmon

used to ascend a great many of the freshwater streams of the Atlantic seaboard in gratifying numbers, Now, of course, there are fewer salmon than there used to be, and the number of streams in which they spawn has been severely reduced. This is true for at least three reasons:

1. With increasing industrialization, many of the streams became so polluted that salmon could no longer survive in them.

2. Even if the water had not been polluted, the larger streams eventually were blocked by one or more of the dams that an industrialized society is in the habit of building. A salmon can swim up streams of considerable turbulence, leaping from pool to pool if necessary, but even a small dam with a 25-foot drop will prevent the passage of the strongest and most determined salmon.

3. Since mature salmon normally don't ascend rivers except to spawn in the waters where they spent their extreme youth, once access to a particular river or part of a river system has been blocked for a few years (by dams or anything else) salmon coming from that particular hatching-ground will have all died out, and even though the obstacle is eventually removed, the area will not immediately come back into use–it is impossible for a salmon to return to where he hasn't been.

From what we know of the process, it seems probable that if we purified the water, removed all the obstacles, and waited for nature to take its course, the salmon could eventually re-establish themselves in the headwaters, a few individuals of each new generation of mature salmon spawning a little farther upriver each year, but the process would be very slow, possibly requiring centuries. Fortunately, the principles whereby man can accelerate the process are pretty well known.

To re-establish a given river or part of a river system as a spawning-ground (after having established that the water between it and the ocean neither is too badly polluted nor is it blocked by obstacles too great for a mature salmon to bypass on his way upstream), you introduce into the water of the area hatchery-raised salmon which are still young enough to be imprinted by the memory of the particular stretch of stream into which they have been introduced. If all goes well, those which do not succumb to disease, or do not fall prey to kingfishers, seagulls, predatory fish, seals, commercial fishermen, or other threats to salmon well-being, will eventually make their way to the ocean, stay there until they mature, return to the water they have been programmed to recognize, and spawn there. Thereafter, the spawning cycle will be self-sustaining.

Some of the factors leading up to the movement to bring back the salmon were as follows:

1. Air pollution, largely caused by industrial emissions and automobile exhausts, got so bad that it could no longer be ignored, and so, with many moans, groans, and protests from the industries affected, a certain amount of state and federal legislation to alleviate it came into being.

2. The air pollution issue focused public attention as never before on the ecology (the word was known only to scholars until after World War II), and public pressure to improve water quality began to build up as well, assisted somewhat by publicity and civil suits by such organizations as Friends of the Earth, the Sierra Club, and the Appalachian Mountain Club.

3. As long as the primary purpose of the larger rivers of the East Coast was to act as a network of high-class sewers, flushing industrial wastes from their point of origin into the ocean, the hopelessness of bringing back the salmon was evident to one and all, but as soon as the water quality had begun to improve, what had been an idle dream now started to look more reasonable.

One of the problems connected with re-establishing salmon spawning-grounds is the question of what to do with all of those dams in the river. If a salmon is to make his way up a river, and the municipality or power company is not prepared to remove the dam, some way of enabling the salmon to bypass the dam must be provided. You can scoop them out of the river and transport them in tank trucks; you can provide a fish elevator, a device that works for fish more or less like people elevators work for people; or you can install a fish-way.

A fish-way (sometimes called a fish ladder) is essentially a series of connected pools, each slightly higher than the next, so that the salmon, by leaping from one to the other, can bypass the main dam and continue on upstream.

The funny thing about fish-ways is that they are by no means new: here and there along the lower reaches of the Connecticut are the barely discernible ruins of fish-ways about 100 years old. The people alive then may not have been much more considerate of the environment than we have lately been, but they knew that if you put a dam in the river, there would thereafter be no salmon fishing above the dam unless the fish could somehow bypass it. It now appears that, since the mechanics of salmon migration were imperfectly understood, these fish-ways weren't very well engineered, and wouldn't have worked very well, but they were never put to much of a test, because not long after they were installed the water became so polluted that the salmon became fewer and fewer, and eventually failed to show up at all.

One of the things that the builders of the 100-year-old fishways never found out was that you can't just build a fish-way off to one side of the dam and expect the salmon to find it–the salmon tends to seek out the main thrust of the current to swim against, and if the main thrust of the current leads him to the pool below the main dam, he will go to the pool and mill around there, with no more hope of getting to the top of the main dam than a man has of leaping from street level to the top of the Empire State Building. For this reason, fish-ways take a lot of engineering to construct and money to pay for, and so dam-owning power companies would rather not pay to build them if it can be avoided.

Physics teaches us that there is such a thing as inertia, which has been rather undramatically defined as that property of matter whereby objects at rest remain at rest, and objects in motion remain in motion, traveling at the same speed and in the same direction unless halted, deflected, speeded up, or slowed down by some outside force. Inertia apparently applies to human endeavor as well: if human beings have been doing nothing in a given field of endeavor, they often continue to do nothing in that same field of endeavor until jolted into activity by what seems like a disproportionate amount of force, and if they are accustomed to acting in a certain way, they usually continue to act that way for quite a while, often in direct defiance of common sense, and it takes an awful lot of energy to induce them to do something else. In human terms, the pattern of resistance to new ideas normally goes through the following sequence:

1. Ignore the issue.

2. When the issue can no longer be ignored, claim that the innovation suggested is unnecessary, unconstitutional, and unAmerican.

3. When legal and extra-legal pressures have increased to the point at which protest is no longer feasible, delay execution as long as possible.

4. When action can no longer be delayed, take action, and then spend lots of public-relations money pointing out how the action you are taking proves how far-seeing, progressive, and altruistic you are.

Although it is now fashionable to load the entire blame for the present salmonlessness of many of the rivers of the Eastern seaboard onto the shoulders of the power companies, this is not quite fair. It seems that at least some of the dams that are now causing all the trouble were built with the understanding, backed up by state law, that no dam was to be built unless it incorporated in its design a fish-way capable of accommodating any fish that wanted to go upstream–shad, for example, as well as salmon. However, it has long been common knowledge among people who build dams that few states are going to insist on their providing a facility for fish which aren't going to show up anyway, so in at least some cases the state has been consciously or unconsciously guilty of encouraging power companies to ignore state law.

For this reason, it was only to be expected that when pressure from the pro-salmon faction started to build, the first reaction from the power companies was astonishment and indignation. "Who are these nuts, anyway? Where do they get the idea that human well-being must be sacrificed to a few stupid fish? Trouble with those people, they aren't realistic–they just don't think in terms of dollars-and-cents costs."

Of course it wouldn't be just a few fish–with proper management, it would be quite a lot of fish. Moreover, once the system was in operation, it would be pretty much self-sustaining, with relatively modest maintenance costs. And the returns would be incalculable.

The movement to restore salmon to the eastern seaboard seems to be proceeding more or less on schedule. The return of salmon to the Penobscot River in Maine has been established; the return of salmon to the Connecticut River system seems to be taking longer (possibly because of the five dams between the ocean and the headwaters), but "redds"–areas on the river bottom that salmon scoop out as a place in which to deposit and fertilize their eggs–have been observed here and there in the headwaters. The presence of these "redds" seems to indicate that immature salmon planted there some years ago have descended the river as parr, spent at least two years in the ocean, and returned to the waters for which they were "programmed."

It must be borne in mind that science can supplement nature in this matter. In nature, female salmon lay the eggs and male salmon fertilize them; those that hatch and are not devoured by predators get "imprinted" by the particular stretch of water in which the eggs were laid, and this "imprinting" insures that, after they mature, they will return to the same stretch of water and no other to spawn.

Since "imprinting" is something an immature salmon acquires simply by spending a fair amount of time in a particular stretch of water, and does not require that spawning salmon deposit their eggs there, "imprinting" will work just as well if a Fish & Game representative assumes a duty normally carried out by spawning salmon and deposits fertilized salmon eggs in this same stretch of water.

It is possible that you might want to contribute to fish well-being (as well as your own) by stocking and maintaining your own fish pond. Here again, the project may be a little trickier than it at first appears.

A few years ago, a neighbor with a pond on his property wanted to stock it with brook trout. Our state provides low-cost juvenile trout, which can be picked up from any of several distribution centers on a given date; the neighbor was not going to be at home on that date, and so he asked me to pick up the fish and install them in the pond. I picked up the trout, each sealed in its own private swimming pool, a plastic bag filled with water, and, following the directions provided, eased them into the pond.

All went well until a particularly hot day, when the neighbor discovered his trout floating belly-up. Trout need well-oxygenated water, and although the pond is fed by a small stream, it is apparently too small to provide the degree of water oxygenation that trout need.

A better bet for a small pond is a type of fish that can get along with a lot less oxygen–large-mouth bass, for example.

If you stock a pond with large-mouth bass, which are cannibalistic, what will probably happen is that the bigger bass will eat the small bass, and you will wind up with four or five monster bass that are too big to eat each other, all starving to death.

All right, then; how about bluegill, which are not cannibalistic? Here you run into a different problem: bluegill multiply so enthusiastically that, given enough time, the pond will be swarming with bluegill, two years old and two inches long, all starving to death.

The thing to do is to set up a predator/prey situation that will feed the predators and at the same time keep the numbers of the prey in check. Stock the pond with bass and bluegill on a ratio of 1 to 4 or 5, and provide some sort of cover so a reasonable number of bluegill can avoid being eaten. This can be a structure consisting of a row of east-and-west-oriented sticks nailed to a row of north-to-south-oriented sticks, on top of which are nailed another row of east-and-west-oriented sticks, and so on, care being taken to insure that the gaps between the sticks are big enough to accommodate infant bluegill, but too close together to let the bass through.

Drop this contraption into the pond and weigh it down with rocks. In that way, the bluegill will consume worms, bugs, spiders, and other small creatures, and the bass will consume the supernumerary bluegill.

Some of the organizations that concern themselves with the future of sport fishing are listed below. You may want to lend your support to one or another of them, depending on the kind of fishing you prefer. If you find that Trout Unlimited discriminates unfairly in favor of trout, or that Salmon Unlimited discriminates unfairly in favor of salmon, to the detriment of other species, you may prefer the Federation of Fly Fishers, but if you find that this organization discriminates unfairly in favor of flies, to the detriment of other lures and baits, you may prefer the Izaak Walton League, which wisely keeps its preferences (if it has any) out of its title.

Salmon Unlimited
4548 North Milwaukee Avenue
Chicago, IL 60634

Federation of Fly Fishers
P.O. Box 1595
Bozeman, MT 59771

Trout Unlimited
1500 Wilson Boulevard
Suite 310
Arlington, VA 22209

Izaak Walton League of America
IWLA Conservation Center
707 Conservation Lane
Gaithersburg, MD 20878

14. The Law

You don't need a license to fish in the ocean,* but inland waters come under the jurisdiction of the states in which they are found, so in inland waters you do. Fishing laws tend to be almost as windy as any other kind, so in most states, the Fish & Game Department publishes a little booklet which sums up just about everything you will need to know about seasons, creel limits, legal and illegal equipment, restrictions on certain waters, and the like.

If you find the regulations unreasonable or unduly complicated, don't blame the Fish & Game Department. Their job is not to write the laws but to enforce them, and they may not approve of everything in the booklet either. This state of affairs comes about, not because legislators are necessarily less intelligent or considerate than Fish & Game officials, but because of the way the law works.

A Fish & Game official tends to be pretty well informed about the latest developments in fish and game management, and hence is usually about 40 or 50 years ahead of general public knowledge. A state legislator not only cannot be as well informed about the subject as the Fish & Game expert, but is also obliged to take into consideration the wishes of his constituents, who are a part of that same less-well-informed public. (This is not to say that a legislator must automatically produce what his constituents clamor for–a politician has been defined as a person who gives the voter what he says he wants, while a statesman tries to find out what is in the voter's best interest, and then persuade him to ask for it–but a legislator would not be human if he did not try to please his constituents as often as he reasonably can.)

For instance, suppose there is a state law requiring that undersized fish of certain species, including bluegill, be returned to the water if caught. Sounds reasonable. The fisherman doesn't really want a runty fish, and for every fish removed from the water while young, there is one fewer that can grow to maturity.

But bluegill don't work that way. Bluegill multiply with more speed than discretion, so that, in the absence of enough predatory fish like bass and pike to thin their numbers, the lakes and ponds in which they live tend to

---

* Today some states do require a salt water license. In some cases (Florida) if you hire a boat guide for the day you are covered, but not if you fish on your own.

build up enormous populations of bluegill, several years old and two or three inches long, competing against each other for food and on the verge of starving to death. For this reason, it is almost universally true that the fisherman who feeds his catch of undersized bluegill to his cats is practicing better conservation than the one who returns them to the water.

The Fish & Game people know all this, but selling the idea to the legislature is another matter. Assuming that a particular legislator sees the point and is in complete agreement, you still may not get your amendment. The first law of politics is survival–the legislator can't do any good if he is voted out of office–and if the legislator knows that his constituents tend to be pretty emotional about infant fish, he may well decide that having the waters of his state swarming with runty bluegill is a small price to pay for a good housing bill, or a minimum wage law, or whatever it is he is primarily interested in.

With this in mind, the fisherman can approach the law from either of two points of view: it is either a damned nuisance to be put up with if necessary and contravened whenever it is convenient and nobody is looking, or it is something else.

Personally, I think it is something else. After all, there is no such thing as a law that doesn't inconvenience somebody somehow, and if everybody obeyed only the laws that happened to suit his convenience, there would be no point in law at all. In the real world, you don't have a choice between perfection (your version of what the law ought to say) and imperfection (what the law actually says)–the real choice is between imperfection and chaos. The good sportsman, like the good citizen, evaluates his objections as they come along–if something to which he objects is a minor nuisance, he ignores it; if it is really important, he fires off an indignant letter to his congressman. If it isn't important enough to do anything about, it isn't important.

Sources Referred To In This Book

CARSON, Rachel, *The Sea Around Us*, Oxford University Press, 1950.

CARSON, Rachel, *Silent Spring*, Houghton Mifflin, 1962.

HEMINGWAY, Ernest, *The Old Man and the Sea*, Charles Scribner's Sons, New York, 1952.

HEYERDAHL, Thor, *Kon-Tiki* (translated by F. H. Lyon), Rand, McNally & Co., Chicago, 1964.

HOYT, Murray, *30 Miles for Ice Cream*, The Stephen Greene Press, Brattleboro, Vermont, 1974.

MOWAT, Farley, *Never Cry Wolf*, Dell Publishing Co., 1963.

WALTON, Izaak, *The Compleat Angler*, Weathervane Books, New York (no date; originally written in 1653).

The best bibliography of sources on sports fishing I know of is Arnold Gingrich's *The Joys of Trout* (Crown Publishers, Inc., New York, edition of 1974), which contains (p. 251 *et ff.*) "Fifty Books for a Fly Fisherman" and "Bibliography: Selective and Supplemental."

If the reader finds Gingrich too partial to trout and salmon, to the exclusion of other fish, and to fly-fishing, to the exclusion of other methods of angling, he can consult the entry under FISHING in Volume I of *Subject Guide to Books in Print*, which lists almost 200 titles. *Books in Print* is published by R. R. Bowker Co., New York and London, with revisions appearing from time to time–the one I have used is the edition of 1976. It is on file at most public libraries.

Index